Van Gogh
and the
Post-Impressionists
for Kids · 21 Activities

Their Lives and Ideas

Carol Sabbeth

CHICAGO REVIEW PRESS

Library of Congress Cataloging-in-Publication Data

Sabbeth, Carol, 1957–
　　Van Gogh and the Post-Impressionists for kids : their lives and ideas, 21 activities / Carol Sabbeth.—1st ed.
　　　　p. cm.
　　　　Includes bibliographical references and index.
　　　　ISBN 978-1-56976-275-2 (pbk.)
　　　　1. Post-impressionism (Art)—Juvenile literature. 2. Gogh, Vincent van, 1853–1890—Friends and associates—Juvenile literature. 3. Art, French—19th century—Juvenile literature. I. Title.
　　　　N6465.P6S23 2011
　　　　709.03'46—dc22

　　　　　　　　　　　　　　　　　　　　　　　　　　　　2010053908

Cover and interior design: Joan Sommers Design
Interior illustrations: TJ Romero

© 2011 by Carol Sabbeth
All rights reserved
First edition
Published by Chicago Review Press, Incorporated
814 North Franklin Street
Chicago, Illinois 60610
ISBN 978-1-56976-275-2
Printed in China
5　4　3　2　1

About the Author

CAROL SABBETH presents art workshops to children and teachers throughout the United States and in England and France. She also performs as a storyteller, bringing art history to life by impersonating famous women artists. She is author of *Frida Kahlo and Diego Rivera*, *Monet and the Impressionists for Kids*, *Crayons and Computers*, and *Kids' Computer Creations*. She lives in Roswell, Georgia, with her husband, Alex.

FRONT COVER IMAGES: Vincent van Gogh, *Self-Portrait*, 1887, Photograph by Robert Hashimoto / Art Institute of Chicago; Henri de Toulouse-Lautrec, *Moulin Rouge, La Goulue*, 1891, Art Institute of Chicago; Paul Gauguin, *Piti Teina (Two Sisters)*, 1892, Hermitage Museum, St. Petersburg; Georges Seurat, *A Sunday on La Grande Jatte, 1884*, 1884–86, Art Institute of Chicago

BACK COVER IMAGE: Vincent van Gogh, *Cafe-Terrace at Night (Place du Forum in Arles)*, 1888, Rijksmuseum Kroeller-Mueller, Photo Credit: Erich Lessing / Art Resource, NY

To Alex

Contents

Acknowledgments

THIS BOOK BEGAN as an answer to a 10-year-old's question. While I was visiting a classroom to talk about the Impressionists, a boy asked me, "Were Monet and van Gogh ever friends?" It made me wonder: Did the red-bearded artist, who is famous for being a loner, have many artist friends? Several people in the United States, the Netherlands, and France have helped me discover the answer. Christine Perreux was my French connection. Hedy Vrakking advised me on all things Dutch. The museum staff at the Vincent van Gogh House in Zundert shared their knowledge about the artist's childhood, as well as his 150th birthday celebration. Many thanks to Karen Ku, Kim Fredrickson, Ruthie Kirk, and the reference librarians at Emory University's Woodruff Library. Thanks also to my editors Lisa Reardon and Michelle Schoob, to Cynthia Sherry, and to my wonderful husband, Alex, for his help and support. Last but not least, to all the children—you come up with the most amazing questions.

Time Line

1848   Paul Gauguin born in Paris on June 7

1853   Vincent van Gogh born in Zundert, the Netherlands, on March 30

1857   Theo van Gogh born on May 1

1863   Paul Signac born in Paris on November 11

1864   Henri de Toulouse-Lautrec born in Albi, France, on November 24

1867   The Paris World's Fair introduces Japanese art to the West

1868   Émile Bernard born in Lille, France, on April 28

1869   Van Gogh starts apprenticeship at art gallery in The Hague

1873   Van Gogh is transferred to London branch of art gallery

1874   First Impressionist exhibition

1875   Van Gogh is transferred to Paris branch of art gallery

1876   Van Gogh becomes schoolteacher in England

1878   Toulouse-Lautrec breaks his leg at age 13. Breaks second leg one year later.

1879   Van Gogh preaches in the Borinage

1880   Van Gogh decides to become an artist and practices drawing on his own

       Gauguin exhibits with the Impressionists

1881   Van Gogh returns to live with his parents and falls in love with his cousin

       Pablo Picasso is born

1885 Van Gogh paints
The Potato Eaters

1886 Van Gogh moves to Paris,
meets Toulouse-Lautrec and
Émile Bernard

Bernard begins walking tour
through Brittany

1887 Signac meets van Gogh at
Tanguy's art supply store

1888 Van Gogh moves to Arles,
France. Gauguin joins him
there. After weeks of tension,
van Gogh has a breakdown and
cuts off part of his ear.

1889 Van Gogh voluntarily enters a
mental asylum, where he paints
The Starry Night

1890 Van Gogh sells his first
and only painting,
The Red Vineyard

In May, he moves to Auvers-
sur-Oise, paints *Portrait of
Dr. Gachet*

Van Gogh shoots himself and
dies two days later at age 37

1891 Gauguin moves to Tahiti

1899 Toulouse-Lautrec commited to
a mental asylum

1901 Toulouse-Lautrec dies at
age 36

1903 Gauguin dies in Hiva Oa at
age 54

1928 Andy Warhol is born

1935 Signac dies in Paris at age 71

1939 World War II begins; Van
Gogh's paintings hidden in
bunkers on the Dutch coast

1941 Bernard dies in Paris at age 72

1973 Van Gogh Museum opens in
Amsterdam

1990 Van Gogh's *Portrait of
Dr. Gachet* sells for record
$82.5 million

2003 Worldwide, people turn
out to celebrate van Gogh's
150th birthday

VINCENT VAN GOGH

Sunflowers, 1888

Vincent and His Colorful Friends

IMAGINE TAKING A STROLL through a field of sunflowers in the south of France. A hundred or so years ago you might have run into a red-bearded artist in a big straw hat standing in front of an easel. He would quickly cover his canvas with thick layers of paint. His colors would be so vivid they'd seem to glow. And oh, how he loved the color yellow! When he was finished, he'd carry the wet canvas to his yellow house, setting it against a wall to dry.

At dinnertime, you might spy him again at a table in the local café. He'd be having a lively discussion with his buddy the postman or writing a letter to his brother Theo. Then again, the letter might be to one of his artist friends. He loved to write letters. On he would go, page after page, writing about everything—but especially about his paintings. Who would have guessed that one day those letters would be read by thousands? Or that his paintings would hang in the greatest museums in the world? Or that the painter, Vincent van Gogh, would be one of the most famous artists who ever lived?

Most of the time van Gogh worked alone. But during a brief time in Paris, he met other young, enthusiastic artists. They all admired the work of the modern Impressionists like Claude Monet. But van Gogh and his peers wanted to take the Impressionists' ideas a step further. The friends painted together, shared their ideas, and enjoyed the nightlife of Paris. They were a talented bunch. Over the years, their ideas were turned into magnificent paintings. These artists came to be called the Post-Impressionists.

This book follows the path of van Gogh and four of his friends—Paul Gauguin, Henri de Toulouse-Lautrec, Paul Signac, and Émile Bernard. It tells the story of their lives and how those lives crossed paths.

Each artist had his own individual style and idea about what to paint. Van Gogh went to southern France to paint the bright blue skies and yellow fields. After a brief stay in southern France, Gauguin moved to Tahiti to capture its tropical landscape. Signac sailed his boat in the Mediterranean Sea and recorded the scene in dazzling dots. Bernard toured the French countryside on foot, painting pictures and writing poetry along the way. Toulouse-Lautrec was happiest sitting in a Paris café, sketching the nightlife that was the subject of his fabulous paintings and posters.

What made their work different from what was painted before? How did the artists help one another? Did they always get along? You'll learn about these things and more while making fun projects along the way. Learn how to paint a self-portrait like van Gogh and make a 3-D peep box of his *Starry Night*. Follow the steps to design a poster like those by Toulouse-Lautrec. Celebrate Signac's two passions by making a Pointillist sailboat (that you can sail!). Write a poem like Bernard, and cook up a soup that's better than van Gogh's. Perhaps you'll find terms that are new to you. If so, look them up in the glossary at the back of the book.

Van Gogh and his friends lived during an exciting time in the history of art. Learn why their paintings are so well loved today.

VINCENT VAN GOGH

Self-Portrait, 1889

1 Happy Birthday, Vincent

ALL BIRTHDAY PARTIES are fun, but the one celebrated on March 30, 2003, takes the cake. It was the 150th anniversary of Vincent van Gogh's birth, and it seemed like the whole world wanted to join in.

Museums in London, Paris, Chicago, and New York celebrated the day with cake, candles, and special events. Every party had balloons, but one balloon was outstanding. In the Dutch village of Zundert, where van Gogh was born, a hot-air balloon decorated with his portrait floated across the countryside, peering down on the festivities.

All this for an artist who was barely acknowledged during his lifetime. He only sold one painting! What would van Gogh have thought?

In Amsterdam, musicians played for hundreds of Dutch families who waited in line at the Van Gogh Museum. Inside, a huge birthday cake dazzled the guests, along with an exhibit designed specially for Vincent. Called *Vincent's Choice*, it displayed van Gogh's favorite works of art. Gathered together from many museums, the exhibit contained works by Rembrandt, Claude Monet, and other famous artists whom van Gogh admired. Shining brightly among these paintings were his own. "It was conceived as a sort of a birthday gift for Vincent," said the museum's director, John Leighton. "We hope it would have made him smile."

A short ride away in Otterlo, another museum displayed over 100 of van Gogh's paintings and drawings. Included were a few works that have been officially recognized as fakes. Knowing that his work was so well loved that it was forged—now *that* would make him smile.

GROWING UP IN HOLLAND

Vincent van Gogh was born on March 30, 1853, in Zundert, a small village near the Belgian border. His father, Theodorus, was a minister. On the day of his son's birth, Reverend van Gogh walked across the square to the town hall, opened the birth register, and proudly wrote "Vincent Willem van Gogh." Sadly, there was already an entry for that same name. Exactly one year earlier Anna van Gogh had given birth to the first Vincent. That baby had been stillborn. A year later the arrival of a healthy son was wonderful news. In the following years two brothers and three sisters would be added to Vincent's family.

Anna van Gogh came from a large family herself. Mrs. van Gogh had seven brothers and sisters. Her father was a talented craftsman, a bookbinder by trade. He was an artist as well. In his free time he liked to sketch flowers and plants, filling notebooks with his drawings. Vincent's mother inherited this talent. Like her father, she enjoyed sketching and watercolor painting.

Theodorus, Vincent's father, came from a family of 11 children. As a young man, Theodorus decided to follow in his father's footsteps and become a minister too. Theodorus was known by the people in his church as the Handsome Pastor. He did have good looks, but many found his long sermons boring. Still, his congregation faithfully came every Sunday to the Dutch Reformed church where he preached. Unfortunately for Reverend van Gogh, the southern area of the Netherlands where they lived was mostly populated by Catholics. As a result, Reverend van Gogh's church had only 120 members. He didn't make a very large income.

Reverend van Gogh's brothers, however, were wealthy businessmen. Three of his five brothers owned art galleries. His most successful sibling, also named Vincent, worked with a French firm with headquarters in Paris. Uncle "Cent" sold works painted by Holland's most popular artists.

A FRECKLED BOY

Young Vincent was a freckled boy with red hair and blue-green eyes. As a youth, Vincent loved to wander through the fields and heaths around his home. This region, or province, of the Netherlands is called North Brabant. The village where he lived was surrounded by small farms, and the families who owned them were poor. Men and women, wearing wooden shoes to keep their feet dry as they sloshed through the mud, worked very hard to earn a living. Vincent had great respect for these peasants and would remember them later in his art.

As a boy, Vincent wasn't particularly interested in art. He showed some talent, but when his parents praised him, he often destroyed his work. He tore up a drawing of a cat climbing a tree when his mother and father admired it too much. An elephant made out of clay was smashed for the same reason. Vincent didn't think his artwork deserved the attention his parents gave it, and he told them so. In later years, what Mrs. van Gogh remembered most about her son was not his artistic talent but his stubborn, willful personality.

As the oldest child, he was the first to attend school in the village. But his days as a schoolboy didn't last long. Most of the other students were farmer's children and must have been too spirited for the van Goghs. When Vincent's parents started to worry that the peasant children were making their son too rough, they took him out of school. Instead, they kept him at home and hired a governess to teach all their children. When Vincent was 11, his parents sent him to a boarding school in a nearby town. Although his parents visited him on occasion, he was sad to be away from home at such a young age.

Vincent was an average student—intelligent but not brilliant. He enjoyed his classes in calligraphy and drawing but didn't think of art as a career. In the 1800s drawing was part of any well-educated young person's training. What Vincent did excel at was languages. He could speak Dutch, German, French, and English. He also loved to read.

When he returned home during vacations, Vincent spent as much time as possible outdoors. He loved nature and explored the hills and dales outside of town, hoping to make new discoveries. He knew where the most beautiful flowers bloomed and could locate the nests of his favorite birds. His younger brothers and sisters would have liked to join him on these outings, but

VINCENT VAN GOGH
The Siesta (after Millet), 1889–90

they didn't dare ask to come along. Their brother was serious, silent, and thoughtful. They knew he preferred to be alone.

When he turned 15, Vincent left school. Like most young men his age, it was time for him to decide on a trade. Once decided, he would begin with an apprenticeship. The trade he chose turned out to be a very good choice for a future artist.

Make Pannekoeken

Children in the Netherlands love these Dutch pancakes, called pannekoeken. They are delicious!

ADULT SUPERVISION REQUIRED

INGREDIENTS

2 tablespoons butter
½ cup milk
2 eggs
½ cup flour
2 tablespoons sugar
½ teaspoon cinnamon

UTENSILS

Oven
Pie pan
Large mixing bowl
Whisk
Measuring cups and spoons
Bowl
Spoon
Oven mitts

1. Preheat the oven to 450°F.
2. Put the butter into the pie pan and place the pan in the oven until the butter melts. Remove the pan and set it aside.
3. In a large bowl, whisk the milk, eggs, and flour together until the batter is smooth.
4. Pour the batter into the buttered pie pan.
5. Mix the sugar and cinnamon in a bowl and sprinkle the mixture over the batter.
6. Bake it in the oven for 15 minutes. Do not open the oven door until the time is up. The pancake will be puffy and golden brown when done.
7. Cut into wedges and serve warm.

Try This Style: Peel and core an apple, and cut it into thin slices. Layer the slices over the batter, sprinkle it with sugar and cinnamon, and bake for 15 minutes.

4

THE YOUNG APPRENTICE

Vincent was going to learn the trade of selling art. He moved 60 miles away, to a city called The Hague, to become an apprentice at his uncle Cent's art gallery. Cent's firm, Goupil & Cie., also had galleries in London, Brussels, New York, and Paris.

The Hague was very different from the farming village where Vincent had grown up. Surrounded by woods and situated right next to the sea, the town provided many new places for him to explore. The city dates back to 1248, when a nobleman built a castle in the forest that he used for hunting. A town developed around the castle and came to be called The Hague, which means "The Hedge." In the 1500s, it became the seat of government for the Netherlands. In van Gogh's day, King William III and the royal family lived there.

In July 1869, 16-year-old Vincent began work as a clerk at the art gallery. Located on a fashionable square called the Plaats, the gallery looked more like the parlor of an opulent mansion than a store that sold paintings. Lush draperies trimmed with tassels hung from windows and decorated the doorways between rooms. The rooms were decorated with expensive furnishings, oriental carpets, and fireplaces graced with beautiful mantels. Most spectacular of all were the paintings. Set in ornate gold frames, they covered the walls from floor to ceiling. The gallery was designed to resemble an upper-class Victorian parlor so buyers could see how the paintings would look in their own homes.

Vincent entered the art trade at the perfect time. The fact that there were so many people who could afford to purchase paintings was relatively new. Previously, the only people wealthy enough to buy artwork were a privileged group of very successful businessmen, kings, queens, and royal-court members. Churches, which were supported by the wealthy, could also commission great works of art. The Industrial Revolution, which was going strong by 1869, changed all that. Railroads were built, large factories were opened, and the businesses that supplied them sprung up throughout Europe. As a result, an upper middle class made up of successful business owners and merchants emerged. They had money to spend on beautiful homes and needed artwork to decorate their walls.

At the time, the most popular paintings were reproduced by a technique called engraving. The Goupil gallery carried these high-quality prints. Vincent was soon assigned the job of selling them. He took his job seriously and eventually became a connoisseur. To do this, he had to study art from ancient times through modern days. He learned all he could about the engravings and the original paintings. Vincent also made a point to meet the many successful Dutch artists who visited the gallery and talk to them about painting.

Everyone at Goupil & Cie., including Vincent, was happy with his progress. During his free time he learned more about his trade by visiting museums and other galleries. His uncle Cor owned a gallery in Amsterdam, which was only 33 miles from The Hague. When not

WHAT'S IN A NAME?

HOLLAND OR THE NETHERLANDS—what should van Gogh's homeland be called? It depends on whom you ask.

Properly speaking, the country where van Gogh was born is called the Kingdom of the Netherlands. Or, as he would say in his native language, "Koninkrijk der Nederlanden." The short version, the Netherlands, means "low land." It is low! Much of the country is below sea level. Without dikes, nearly half the country would be underwater. The name Holland means "land in a hollow." Technically, this name only applies to a section of the country: 2 of the 12 provinces, called North Holland and South Holland. This is where the cities of Amsterdam, Delft, and The Hague are. The Dutch prefer to call their country "Nederland." It is English-speaking people who often refer to the country as Holland.

Why are people from the Netherlands called Dutch? This comes from the German word "Deutsch," which means German. Originally the English used the word to refer to all Germanic people (people from Germany, Switzerland, and the Netherlands). In the 16th century, due to trading, the English were most often in contact with Hollanders. The name "Dutch" came to be limited to the people of the Netherlands.

Letter from Vincent to Paul Gauguin from Arles, France, October 17, 1888

visiting his uncle, Vincent spent hours exploring the great art museums there, where he could study the paintings of Dutch and Flemish masters such as Jan Vermeer, Frans Hals, and Rembrandt. It's common for aspiring artists to set up easels in front of such great works and practice the painting techniques of the masters. But this didn't occur to Vincent. At the time he had no intention of becoming an artist. If he sketched at all, it was to take notes or explain an idea.

Three years after Vincent moved to The Hague, his brother Theo came to visit. Theo, who was four years younger, looked just like Vincent. Theo was thrilled to spend time with his older brother. He would soon need to begin an apprenticeship, and it turned out that he would follow the same path as his brother.

A few days after Theo went home, Vincent wrote to thank him for visiting. It was the beginning of a friendship they maintained through letters. In the years to come, Vincent would write more than 600 letters to Theo.

Six months after his visit, Theo started his apprenticeship at Goupil & Cie. The company's mangers didn't want brothers working at the same gallery, so Theo was sent to the branch in Brussels, Belgium. Soon after, Vincent was transferred to London to get experience at the English branch of the company. After four successful years at the gallery, it was a promotion to be proud of. The director of The Hague branch, Mr. Tersteeg, wrote to Vincent's parents telling them how much his clients, as well as painters, enjoyed working with their son.

ON TO LONDON

In May 1873, 20-year-old van Gogh arrived in England. He loved London and enjoyed strolling through its beautiful parks and gardens. One of his favorite places to visit was Hyde Park, where "hundreds of ladies and gentlemen ride on horseback." Because he spoke fluent English, he had no problem communicating with the people he met. He was a successful salesman, and the gallery paid him well. He could be seen in top hat and gloves, like the other gentlemen of the city.

He found a room in a boardinghouse within walking distance of his new job. There was a piano in the parlor, and it was a cheery, welcoming place. The woman who owned the home, Ursula Loyer, was a clergyman's

My dear Theo,

I'm getting on very well here. I've got a delightful home and I'm finding it very pleasurable taking a look at London and the English way of life and the English people themselves, and then I've got nature and art and poetry, and if that isn't enough, what is? But I haven't forgotten Holland and especially not The Hague and Brabant.

Vincent

— Letter from Vincent van Gogh to Theo van Gogh (excerpt), London, January 1874

VAN GOGH'S LETTERS

VINCENT VAN GOGH was an excellent letter writer. Luckily for us, his brother Theo was an excellent collector. Vincent often had a difficult time communicating with people face-to-face. But when he took up his pen, his ideas flowed. He wrote about everything: his favorite books, the artists who inspired him, his ups and downs. He often included sketches to illustrate his words. Most of his letters were to Theo, but letters to other family members, friends, and artists still exist. Theo kept all his letters in a desk drawer. His wife, Jo, remembered watching the pile of yellow envelopes with Vincent's familiar handwriting quickly stack up. Later, after both brothers had died, Jo carefully documented the letters. Then she shared them. Today, much of what is known about Vincent's ideas comes from the letters he wrote.

A Picture in Words

When van Gogh became an artist, he enjoyed roaming the countryside with his easel strapped to his back, looking for interesting scenes. The Red Vineyard depicts one sight he came across while in southern France. It was the only painting by van Gogh that sold during his lifetime. Before Theo ever saw the painting, he had a good idea what it looked like. The first news of it came in a letter. Practice seeing a scene as van Gogh would have. Then write a letter to a friend describing it.

MATERIALS

Pencil or pen

Writing paper

Envelope

Address of a friend

Postage stamp

1. Choose an outdoor scene that you'd like to tell a friend about. You could describe a baseball game or a beach scene, for instance.

2. While you are at the setting, pay close attention to the colors and shapes that you see. Observe your scene for at least 10 minutes. The longer you look, the more you will notice.

My dear Theo,

But on Sunday if you had been with us, you would have seen a red vineyard, all red like red wine. In the distance it turned to yellow, and then a green sky with the sun, the earth after the rain violet, sparkling yellow here and there where it caught the reflection of the setting sun.

Ever yours, Vincent

— Letter from Vincent van Gogh to Theo van Gogh (excerpt), Arles, on or about November 3, 1888

Here are some things to look for:

• What is the light like? Are there interesting shadows? Perhaps the sun is low, and the shadows are long. Or it might be foggy, making things a little out of focus.

• Are there reflections? The surface of a lake or puddle might reflect the clouds above.

• Look for subtle color differences. For instance, is the color of the sky different than that of the water?

3. Write a letter describing what you see. Give details about the scene. For instance, instead of saying

something is "pretty," describe what it is that makes it pretty. Use comparisons to describe a color. For example, instead of "yellow," you might write "as yellow as an egg yolk."

4. After your written description, make a sketch of your scene.

5. Mail your letter to a friend.

Try Another Style: Ask your friend to paint a picture of the scene you described. She can include it in her letter when she writes back to you. Then she can add a description of a scene for you to paint.

VINCENT VAN GOGH

The Red Vineyard at Arles,
1888

widow, and van Gogh felt comfortable with her motherly ways. In the evenings, he enjoyed the company of his fellow lodgers. In a letter to Theo he wrote, "There are also three German boarders who are very fond of music, they play the piano and sing, so we spend very pleasant evenings together."

Mrs. Loyer's 19-year-old daughter Eugénie also lived at the house. Along with helping her mother with their boarders, she ran a nursery school for young children. It wasn't long before van Gogh fell madly in love with her. Eugénie, who wasn't aware of his infatuation, treated him kindly. But she didn't treat him like a boyfriend.

In fact, she was secretly engaged to a former boarder. Later, van Gogh's sister Anna came to stay at the home while looking for a job as a teacher. She noticed her brother's infatuation immediately. The fact that he denied it didn't stop her from reporting the news home to their family.

After a year at the boardinghouse, van Gogh could no longer keep his secret. He declared his love and asked Eugénie to marry him. Even though he was persistent, she rejected him.

Van Gogh was devastated. His whole outlook on life changed, and he became silent and moody. The dramatic change in his personality showed in his workplace, too. The young man whom clients and artists had enjoyed so much was now impossible to get along with. He and Anna moved to another home, but his spirits didn't lift. Hoping a change of scene would cheer him up, Uncle Cent arranged for him to be transferred to Paris—the art capital of the world.

THE CITY OF LIGHT

Van Gogh arrived in France in May 1875 to work at one of the Paris branches of Goupil & Cie. The move, however, did not turn out as Uncle Cent had hoped.

Instead of enjoying Paris, as most 22-year-olds would, van Gogh shut himself up in his room to read and discuss the Bible with a young Englishman who also worked at the gallery. For the first time since he left home, he began attending church regularly. His letters to Theo and his family included long passages from the sermons he heard. In the past, his letters often ended with news about a book by a favorite author, like Charles Dickens. Now he warned Theo to stop reading everything except the Bible. Because his behavior was drastically different, it worried his family. Even his father, who was a minister, worried that van Gogh was becoming a fanatic.

At the gallery, van Gogh started quarreling with customers. He spoke rudely to them, challenging their taste. At Christmas he was anxious to go home to his family. Van Gogh knew it was the busiest time of the year for the gallery but left anyway, without permission. When he returned after the holidays, he was fired. His boss, Mr. Boussod, generously gave him three month's notice. Not even Uncle Cent could fix the mess van Gogh found himself in. After seven years as an art dealer, van Gogh was out of a job.

He was ready for a change. Lately he had found everything connected with business more and more distasteful. Ready to follow a new path, van Gogh announced that "there were no professions in the world other than those of schoolmaster and clergyman."

On his last day at the gallery, van Gogh received a reply to his application for a job as a teaching assistant in England. The offer came from a man who ran a boarding school for poor boys between the ages of 10 and 14. Mr. Stokes, who was "completely bald and wears whiskers," agreed to give van Gogh food and lodging as payment, but no salary.

LIFE AS A SCHOOLMASTER

Van Gogh arrived in England eager to start his new career. His school was in Ramsgate, a village on the southeastern coast. The school had a stunning view of the sea and faced a square that had a large lawn surrounded by lilac bushes.

Despite the school's picturesque surroundings, however, things weren't so pleasant there. A room in the living quarters where the boys washed had rotten floorboards and broken windows. The cold wind from the sea whistled in, and cockroaches were everywhere.

Just two months after his arrival, van Gogh wanted a change. He liked teaching but couldn't continue without a salary. Still filled with religious zeal, he hoped to find a salaried position where his duties would include teaching Bible stories. It wasn't long before he found what seemed like the perfect solution. In a village near London, the director of a religious school needed a teacher who would be willing to perform many duties. He would receive a meager salary of 2 pounds, 10 shillings a month. It was one-third of what he had earned in London as an art dealer.

Van Gogh worked very hard for his small salary; he taught languages and Bible history, weeded the garden, tutored, and acted as the school's bill collector. Once in a while, to his delight, he was allowed to give a sermon. Unfortunately, he had inherited his father's poor speaking skills. And the sermons he wrote were depressing. His first, which read in part, "Sorrow is better than joy. . . . It is better to go to the house of mourning than to the house of feasts," wasn't a hit. The audience response, however, didn't dampen his enthusiasm.

At Christmas, he went home to his family and informed them that he had found his true mission in life; like his father and grandfather, he would be a clergyman.

Reverend van Gogh wasn't so sure the job suited his son, but if Vincent wished it, he would help. But first, he thought, his son needed proper training. He needed to become an ordained minister. As an official representative of the church, he could get a proper job.

Becoming ordained, however, required that van Gogh attend theology school.

VINCENT VAN GOGH

Head of a Peasant Woman, 1884

2 Becoming an Artist

VAN GOGH HAD A LOT of work ahead of him. To be ordained in the Dutch Reformed Church required six years of diligent study. First, he had to pass a state entrance exam to get into theology school. Although van Gogh spoke four languages, he needed a tutor to learn Latin and Greek.

Van Gogh moved in with his uncle's family in Amsterdam and began eagerly studying for the entrance exam with a young rabbi named Mendes da Costa. Van Gogh, who had always been good at languages, didn't mind Latin. But Greek, in his opinion, was a waste of time. Why should he need to know Greek, he wondered, to minister to the poor?

More than anything, van Gogh wanted to help the poor and disadvantaged. Rabbi da Costa knew this firsthand. When van Gogh came to his house for lessons, the student made a point to pay attention to da Costa's deaf brother. His visits were also welcomed by da Costa's elderly, disfigured aunt. When she saw van Gogh coming up the walk, she ran to the door to greet him as fast as her old, short legs allowed. "Good morning, Mister van Gort," she would beam. Van Gogh always had a kind word for her. Later, he told the rabbi, "Mendes, however strangely that aunt of yours pronounces my name, she is a good soul; I rather like her." (The word "gort" is Dutch for "barley groats"!)

In the beginning, van Gogh made good progress. He was quickly able to translate a simple book written in Latin. But when it came to the Greek verbs, he was lost. No matter how da Costa tried to explain them, he couldn't understand.

As time went on, all van Gogh's studies became too difficult. Realizing the hard task he faced, he began to feel anxious. The stress became unbearable.

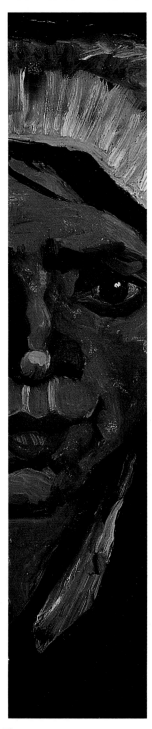

Van Gogh confided in da Costa about how the pressure was affecting him. Thinking himself a failure, he punished himself by beating his body with a stick. Other times during that winter, he locked himself out of his uncle's house and slept on the floor of a cold shed without a blanket.

After a year watching van Gogh struggle, da Costa had to admit that graduating from theology school would be impossible for van Gogh. Van Gogh agreed; it was useless. He couldn't even pass the entrance exam.

Reverend van Gogh tried to come up with an alternative plan. He learned of an evangelical course in Belgium that would be easier. It required less time too—three years of study instead of six. Accompanied by his father, van Gogh went to Brussels to interview at the school. He was accepted into the program on a trial basis.

The trial didn't go well. During the three-month period, Reverend van Gogh received alarming reports that his son was starving himself and sleeping on the floor. Van Gogh was disrespectful to his professors, too. When asked a question in class he once answered, "Sir, I really don't care."

Surprisingly, at the end of his trial period, the school accepted him, but not on the same terms as the other students. They were offered a free education that included room and board, but Van Gogh would have to pay for his food and lodging. Not willing to ask his parents for more money, he dropped out of the course.

Then he found an alternative that suited him perfectly. He was able to convince the church to give him a six-month assignment in the Borinage, a coal mining district in southwestern Belgium. The region was one of the most poverty-stricken areas in the country. Van Gogh's assignment was to spread the church's faith by preaching to the mining families. At last he would be able to do what he dreamed of: minister to the poor.

MINISTERING TO THE MINERS

Van Gogh arrived in the Borinage on Christmas Eve, 1878. It was snowing, and the image he saw when he went to the mine made an impression on him. He watched as the miners came up from the mine covered in coal dust from head to foot. The contrast of their jet-black shapes against the snow at dusk reminded him of the black-and-white etchings he used to sell. Soon he would try to capture these images on paper.

The 25-year-old missionary began his ministry as a respectable representative of the church. He dressed in a dignified fashion, was well groomed, and lodged with the local baker and his wife. Looking like the minister he was hired to be, he threw himself into his duties.

The miners were some of the most deprived workers in Belgium. They worked long, grueling hours 1,500 feet below the ground. To enter a mine, workers rode in a large basket that was lowered by a rope, like a bucket into a well. Occasionally the basket would tip over or fall, killing whoever was riding inside. Children as young as eight years old were forced to descend into the dark pit. Their job was to load coal into the carts that ran on rails along the bottom. Horses, who were kept below and never saw daylight, pulled the carts to an area where the coal was raised to the surface. It was extremely dangerous work. The miners faced poisoned air, cave-ins, and explosions that spread deadly fires. At night, the worn-out workers went home to little huts. Even with their long hours of toil, they barely earned enough money for food and clothes.

Van Gogh's heart went out to these people. Determined to help any way he could, he did much more than preach to them. He gave away his nicely tailored, warm clothes and wore an old soldier's jacket and shabby cap. When accidents happened, he helped take care of the victims. He tore his shirts into strips to use as bandages or dipped the pieces of cloth into olive oil to soothe the burns of miners who had been left to die.

He thought that in order to help the miners, he had to live like them. He couldn't bear to be comfortable when they were not. He moved out of his room at the baker's home and rented a hovel that didn't have furniture. He decided that soap was a sinful luxury and stopped washing the coal dust from his face. He even went down into a mine to better understand what the workers faced.

One day the baker's wife passed van Gogh on the street and chastised him for the way he looked. She reminded him that he came from a noble family of Dutch pastors and should act like one. Other merchants agreed. They thought ministers should be clean, well dressed, and dignified. A minister should be a respectable person they could look up to.

His employer thought so too. When the head of the mission criticized him for his excessive actions and shabby clothes, van Gogh was his usual stubborn self. When his six-month trial period was over, the mission sponsors refused to renew his contract. Once again, he was out of a job.

In October, Theo came to offer his brother practical advice. He tried to convince van Gogh to pursue a different career. Vincent stubbornly refused to listen. The last time he had followed family advice, he had tried to enter theology school. That was a disaster. He sent Theo away and didn't write to him for nine months. The family didn't know how he survived that winter without a job or money. Reverend van Gogh, convinced his son was crazy, tried to have him committed to an insane asylum.

A NEW PLAN

Van Gogh didn't tell his family that he had another plan. Perhaps he kept it a secret because if it didn't work out, he didn't want them to know he failed. Earlier, while working as a preacher, he had started sketching the people he preached to. The sketches, he thought, would help him remember what he saw. That summer he had written to his former boss, Mr. Tersteeg, who was still director of the gallery where Vincent began his apprenticeship. He

VINCENT VAN GOGH

The Carrot Puller, 1885

had asked Tersteeg to send him watercolors, a sketchbook, and two instruction manuals about drawing.

After his dismissal, van Gogh decided to pursue art full steam. He practiced the lessons in the how-to-draw books over and over. His first attempts were stiff and crude. But that didn't stop van Gogh. The one thing he excelled at was persistence. When he got an idea into his head, he didn't give up easily.

After working on a lesson, he applied what he learned to his sketches of miners. Although he was making progress, by winter he started to get discouraged. He knew he needed guidance from a professional artist. A professional, he thought, could see what he was doing wrong and help him correct it.

Van Gogh decided to visit Jules Breton, a French painter whose work he admired. He had met him while working at the Goupil Art Gallery and knew he lived 50 miles away in Courrières, France. Impulsively, without notifying Breton, van Gogh set off by train to pay a visit. Before he got very far, he had to get off the train and continue on foot—the train didn't go to Courrières.

Van Gogh admired Breton's work because he painted scenes of peasants. Breton, van Gogh thought, was an artist he could relate to, someone who shared his ideas about poverty. But when he got to Courrières, he took one look at Breton's large brick house and changed his mind. Van Gogh believed that a painter of poor people should live like one. Breton's home was too luxurious for a painter of peasants, and van Gogh wanted nothing to do with him.

Shades of Gray

One lesson van Gogh was sure to have worked on was "value"—the light, medium, and dark shades in a picture. Make a value scale, then use it while copying van Gogh's drawing of a woman pulling carrots. Don't worry if your end result doesn't look like van Gogh's. Even he had to practice over and over.

MATERIALS

Ruler

2 sheets drawing paper

Pencil

Eraser

Facial tissue

Scissors

1. To make a value scale, draw a rectangle that is 10 inches wide and 2 inches high. Divide the rectangle into 2-inch squares to create 5 sections. Number each section, 1 through 5, below each square.

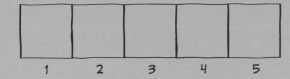

2. Using a pencil, press very softly to make section #1 a very light shade of gray. Blend your strokes by gently rubbing them with a tissue.

3. Press hard to make the last section, #5, very dark.

4. Make section #3 a value that is halfway between the darkest and lightest sections.

5. Make section #2 a value halfway between sections #1 and #3.

6. Make section #4 a value halfway between sections #3 and #5.

7. Trim the paper along the top of the boxes. Place your scale next to van Gogh's drawing *The Carrot Puller*.

8. On a separate piece of paper, make a rough sketch of van Gogh's picture. Do not add shading yet—draw the picture in outline.

9. Compare your value scale to the many shades of gray van Gogh used in his picture. Add the gray tones to your sketch, referring to your scale and van Gogh's drawing as you work.

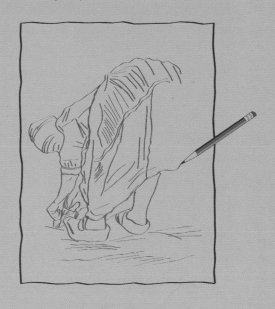

17

During the long walk all the way home, van Gogh was overwhelmed by the beautiful countryside. He saw all the scenes he wished to sketch: farmhouses with mossy, thatched roofs; peasants farming with workhorses; and old women tending their gardens. Even though he didn't achieve what he had set out to do, van Gogh returned home enthusiastic about art. He drew constantly, practicing figures, sketching miners, and copying the work of famous artists from the prints that he owned. He spoke less and less about religion and more and more about art. At age 27, van Gogh set out on his final career: to be an artist.

BECOMING AN ARTIST

Van Gogh packed his belongings and set off for Brussels. He knew he could meet many artists in the large city and hoped they would give him advice. His parents were happy to see their son take a new path and sent an allowance to get him started. With their help, he was able to rent a room in a small hotel.

Some of van Gogh's new plans didn't work out. He applied to the School of Fine Arts but didn't get accepted. He also had trouble finding a job. He hoped his uncles would use their connections to find a position for him, perhaps as a draftsman. This time, they refused to help. They were not willing to do any more favors for their unpredictable nephew.

His brother hadn't given up on him, though. Now working in Paris as a salesman at Goupil, Theo had the means to help, both financially and professionally. He decided that if van Gogh wanted to be an artist, he would help. He'd share his thoughts on art, give his brother moral support, and send him a monthly allowance to buy food and supplies. In return, van Gogh agreed to send Theo his finished work. Along with giving his brother feedback on his art, Theo would try to sell it.

But Theo's small monthly allowance wasn't enough to support Vincent. After buying art supplies, Vincent had nothing left for food. He returned home to live with his parents.

RETURNING HOME

This time, when he returned home, van Gogh did not feel he was a failure. He had a goal and was determined to reach it. His parents, relieved that their son was safe, welcomed him back and encouraged him to continue drawing.

But they had to adjust to his arrival. Van Gogh wasn't willing to change his ways to try to fit in, so his parents did their best to tolerate his personality. He still wore shabby clothes and lacked social skills. They now lived in Etten, where his father was the reverend at a new church. The people in the village surely gossiped about his strange son.

Being back home and having enough food to eat brightened van Gogh's mood. His letters to Theo were lively and cheerful. They no longer contained pages full of Bible verses and sermons. Instead, van Gogh asked about artists he admired and gave details of what he was working on.

Etten is a small village near Zundert, where van Gogh grew up. Just as he did as a boy, he spent his days exploring the countryside. Now he took his easel with him. He sketched the landscape, the thatched cottages where the farmers lived, their barns and ploughs and wheelbarrows.

Everything was going great—until later that summer when a visitor arrived. His cousin from Amsterdam, Kee Vos-Stricker, came to stay at the house, along with her child. Vincent had been friendly with Kee and her husband when he lived in Amsterdam. Recently, Kee's husband had died, leaving her a widow with a small son.

Vincent went out of his way to welcome his cousin. They went on walks together, and van Gogh played games with her little boy. Kee appreciated his hospitality, thinking his kindness was a response to her fatherless son. It wasn't long before Vincent fell head over heels in love with her. When he declared his undying love and asked her to marry him, she was shocked. "No, never, never!" she replied. She packed their bags and fled with her son back to her parents' home in Amsterdam.

Not one to give up, Vincent showered her with letters, which she returned unopened. His parents were aghast at his behavior and pleaded with him to stop the nonsense. But Vincent stubbornly kept up his pleas to Kee. He refused to accept her rejection, even when his parents threatened to throw him out of the house.

Realizing that letters wouldn't work, Vincent decided to go to Amsterdam to pursue her in person. He showed up at the Stricker home during dinnertime and demanded to see Kee. His uncle let him in but told him Kee had run out of the house as soon as she saw him arrive. He chastised his nephew and demanded he stop writing to her. Sitting at the table, van Gogh held his hand over the flame of an oil lamp and said, "Let me see her for as long as I can keep my hand in the flame." Stricker blew out the flame. "You will not see her," he replied. After three days, van Gogh finally gave up and returned to Etten.

Back home, tension remained between van Gogh and his father. It reached a head on Christmas Eve when van Gogh refused to go to church. Their argument grew, ending with the reverend demanding that van Gogh leave the house immediately.

THE HAGUE

Earlier that year, van Gogh had traveled to The Hague to meet other artists. A group of painters who called themselves The Hague School lived there and painted the surrounding landscape. One of the leaders of the group, Anton Mauve, was related to van Gogh through marriage: Mauve's wife, Jet, was van Gogh's cousin. During van Gogh's visit, Mauve had taken an interest in his work. Now van Gogh had returned to ask Mauve for help.

Although Mauve wasn't an easy person to get along with, he generously lent van Gogh money to set up a

VINCENT VAN GOGH

Child Kneeling in Front of a Cradle, 1883

studio in The Hague. With it, he rented a room in a poor part of town, near the train station. He bought a few pieces of furniture and set about decorating his space by covering its walls with art.

Mauve generally didn't give art lessons, but perhaps because van Gogh was his wife's cousin, he agreed to teach him. The lessons began smoothly. Mauve taught him how to paint in watercolor and gave him plaster casts to use for models. Van Gogh admired Mauve, who was an established, successful painter. But after a few months working closely together, van Gogh started to rebel against Mauve's artistic ideas. Specifically, he did not like Mauve's insistence on drawing from plaster casts. Van Gogh preferred to use real people as models. In a fit of anger he smashed some of the casts. When Mauve heard about it, he told van Gogh to stay away for two months.

One day Uncle Cor came to visit van Gogh's studio. He looked at his nephew's sketches and was impressed by three scenes of The Hague's historic district. Uncle Cor felt he could sell these at his gallery. Perhaps a tourist would buy one as a souvenir. He gave him two and a half guilders for each and ordered nine more works to be done in a similar style.

Thrilled with the possibility of earning money with his sketches, van Gogh set to work. But instead of drawing similar scenes of lovely buildings, he chose industrial sights: the local gasworks and the iron foundry. They were not scenes that tourists would want for a happy memory of their visit to Holland. Uncle Cor tried again, being very specific about what he had in mind. This time van Gogh gave him drawings of a fish-drying barn and laundry. He chose industrial scenes because, he claimed, drawing pretty settings hurt his artistic progress. Uncle Cor said they were not salable and canceled his order.

VAN GOGH'S LITTLE FAMILY

One by one, van Gogh lost the support of his friends and family. He knew the real reason: a woman named Christine Hoornik. Christine, who called herself Sien, was living with van Gogh. When he met Sien, she was sick and pregnant. She wasn't married, and to support herself and her five-year-old daughter, she worked at sewing and laundering. She also worked as a prostitute. To van Gogh, she was a sick, poor woman who needed help. To his friends and relatives, she was an uneducated, crude woman of the streets who had a bad temper. When van Gogh asked her to live with him, they were appalled.

The truth was, van Gogh was lonely. The thought of having a little family filled an empty part of his life. To accommodate his new family, he moved to a larger studio just two doors down. His new apartment had well-lighted rooms and a large attic. He hung curtains and built partitions to make it cozy. Sien had her baby, which was a boy. Van Gogh was elated about having a little cradle with a peacefully sleeping baby in it while he

worked. He sketched a touching picture of Sien's little girl rocking the cradle.

In August, Theo came to visit. He also was not thrilled with his brother's living arrangement. The van Goghs were a respectable family, he reminded his brother, not the kind who knew prostitutes, let alone lived with them. Van Gogh refused to listen to Theo's criticisms about his "little family." He defended his lifestyle by arguing that Sien earned her keep by modeling for him and cleaning his studio. It was true that she had a bad temper, he admitted, but that would make her understand his own outbursts.

Theo thought the whole arrangement was disgraceful. But he still continued to support his brother, and now his "little family" as well. As time went on, it became clear that the money he sent couldn't support four people. As Sien regained her health, she demanded more time and money from van Gogh. Her mother, who also wanted to be supported, urged her to go back to work as a prostitute. She could earn more money being a prostitute, her mother argued, than she did being an artist's model.

After eighteen months with Sien, van Gogh began to admit that his arrangement wasn't working. He was ready to move on but couldn't bear leaving the children. In a year and a half, he had become very attached to them. But something had to change.

Van Gogh decided to leave The Hague. He asked Sien to join him, but she refused. When he left, he gave

Activity

Lights, Camera, . . . Action!

Pretend you are a movie director who is directing a scene from van Gogh's painting The Potato Eaters. *Learn how make to a "still" of the scene for publicity. Then make a movie based on van Gogh's famous meal.*

MATERIALS

Picture of van Gogh's *The Potato Eaters*
Camera
5 people who will be actors
Table with 4 chairs
Props: teapot, 5 teacups, forks, hats, plate of small potatoes
Optional: video camera

1. Your goal is to re-create van Gogh's scene from *The Potato Eaters*. Begin by carefully studying his painting. Here are some things to look for:
   • Where is each person placed in the picture?
   • Where is each person looking?
   • What action is each person doing?
   • What items are on the table?

2. Set the props on the table, and place the chairs in position.

3. Show van Gogh's painting to the actors who will be posing for the picture. Assign each a character to imitate, and explain how you'd like them to pose. Give them their props, and ask each actor to practice.

4. Arrange the actors around the table.

5. Stand with your camera at the spot where van Gogh would have stood to capture his image. When you are ready to take a photograph, let the actors know they need to strike their pose. Take several shots.

6. Make a print of your favorite shot and frame it for your own version of van Gogh's masterpiece.

Try Another Style: Make a movie or commercial. Write a script or let the actors improvise the scene while you record it with a video camera. Try different approaches—serious, upbeat, and silly. Have a film festival to show your movies, and use your photograph to advertise the event.

her the most valuable thing he had—a piece of his best canvas to make clothes for the children. He set out for Drenthe, a province in the north of Holland known for its beauty.

Because of its inspiring scenery, Drenthe attracted artists. Mauve had painted there, and van Gogh thought its wild, windswept beauty would inspire him too. He arrived in September and was happy to find it as beautiful as he had heard. He thought he would stay forever. But when the autumn colors faded and the rains came, things changed. Because he had to stay indoors, he decided to paint portraits of the local villagers. But he couldn't get anyone to pose for him. They were inhospitable and mistrustful of him because he was an outsider. As winter came, bringing snow and cold, van Gogh got lonely. He packed his bags, loaded up his canvases, and walked to the train station, which was six hours away. He headed home to see his parents.

Van Gogh's parents were now living in Nuenen, another small Brabant village, where his father was now reverend. Van Gogh didn't intend to stay long, but things didn't turn out as he expected.

THE "BIG ROUGH DOG"

The van Goghs were leery about their son's return but made room for him in their home. They even allowed him to turn their laundry room into a studio. Resigned to his odd personality, they decided to let him dress and act as he pleased, even though it would raise eyebrows

22

The Potato Eaters, 1885

in the small village. Van Gogh didn't care what others thought. Visitors who came for dinner witnessed the unmannered artist jumping up from the table to eat his bread in the corner while brooding over an unfinished painting. When he painted outdoors, villagers who peeked over his shoulder were ordered to go away.

Van Gogh was aware of the turmoil he caused for his parents. In a letter to Theo he wrote, "They feel the same dread of taking me in the house as they would about taking in a big rough dog. He would run into the room with wet paws—and he is so rough. He will be in everybody's way. And he barks so loud. In short he is a foul beast."

There were tense moments in the family, but things got better because of an accident. One day Mrs. van Gogh stepped off a train, fell, and broke her leg. When

"THEY WILL SURELY RECOGNIZE MY WORK"

SOME VILLAGERS THOUGHT van Gogh had talent and asked for art lessons. He accepted three students, and they became friends. For payment they gave him tubes of paint.

His students discovered that van Gogh had an unusual method of painting, which was very different from what they learned elsewhere. Before applying paint, he carefully planned out his scene. Then, without making a rough sketch on the canvas, he quickly applied paint using a large brush, his fingers, and even his fingernails.

Later, van Gogh gave one of his favorite paintings to Anton Kerssemakers, one of his pupils. He was wealthy enough to pay for it, but when van Gogh saw how good it looked in his friend's home and how much Kerssemakers liked it, he didn't ask for money. "I felt such a flow of satisfaction when I saw that it was pleasing . . . that I could not sell it," he wrote to Theo. When Kerssemakers pointed out that it wasn't signed, van Gogh replied, "Actually it isn't necessary, they will surely recognize my work later on and write about me when I am dead and gone."

she returned from the hospital, van Gogh surprised everyone. Just as he had done with the injured coal miners, he took charge of his mother's recovery. To his family's amazement, he nursed her with tender care. They were impressed with his skill and dedication.

During his stay in Nuenen, van Gogh focused on drawing and painting peasant life. One evening, after painting outside all day, he passed the cottage of the De Groot family and stepped inside to have a rest. They were just starting their meal, and van Gogh was inspired by the scene. All through that winter, he sketched studies of their hands and heads. Then he purchased a large canvas and painted the family eating under the light of a single lamp that hung overhead. The colors were dark—browns, grays, and greens—highlighted with dabs of white. He painted their heads "the color of a dusty potato, unpeeled of course." They were eating potatoes, and van Gogh wanted people who saw the painting to almost smell the smoke and grease that filled the hut. He titled his painting *The Potato Eaters*.

Van Gogh was certain he had created a masterpiece. Today, *The Potato Eaters* is considered a great painting. But when Theo saw it, he wasn't impressed. He told his brother that a new group of artists in France was painting with much brighter colors. To be successful in Paris, he would have to use less black and "soapy greens." Van Gogh wrote back that he had heard about these artists, called the Impressionists, but he couldn't visualize what Theo was talking about.

More and more, Theo was taking on the role of his brother's art dealer. But van Gogh didn't think his brother was working hard enough to sell his work. After a huge quarrel, a new arrangement was made. Theo agreed to send van Gogh 150 francs each month as a salary. In return van Gogh sent Theo his paintings. Theo could sell them or keep them as he pleased. There would be no pressure for Theo to find buyers. In return, van Gogh would not have to justify how he used his salary. They were business partners.

With his new earnings, van Gogh moved his studio to a larger space in the village. It was next to the Begemann family—an older couple and their 43-year-old daughter, Margot. Margot, who had never been married, liked van Gogh. She accompanied him on his painting expeditions, and before long the two lonely people decided to get married. Their families, however, objected. Margot's three sisters were especially opposed to the idea and browbeat her until she could no longer take it.

One day, while walking with van Gogh in a field, she collapsed. Unknown to van Gogh, she had swallowed strychnine, a poison used to kill rats. Doctors saved her, but given her unstable emotional condition, the marriage was called off. Most of the villagers blamed van Gogh for the ordeal.

MOVING ON

Seven months later, in March 1885, van Gogh's father died of a stroke. Fearing that van Gogh would cause too much stress for their grieving mother, his three sisters asked him to move out of the house. It hurt him to leave, but he obeyed their wishes and moved into his studio. He stayed several months before deciding to leave Nuenen. One reason for his decision was a lack of models. The local priest, who never liked van Gogh, claimed he was a bad influence and forbade his church members to pose for him. He hadn't done anything wrong, but van Gogh knew it was time to leave.

Van Gogh moved to Antwerp, Belgium, where he rented a little room above a paint dealer's shop. Antwerp was full of museums, cafés, and bustling activity. While exploring the city, he discovered a shop near the waterfront that sold inexpensive prints from Japan. He admired their colorful, flat shapes and bought some to decorate the walls of his room. Van Gogh thought the prints were fascinating. They began to show up in the background of his own work.

In January, he enrolled in the Academy of Fine Arts. The classes were free and offered live models to work from. The teachers, however, were a problem. They didn't understand van Gogh's talent, thinking his work was sloppy. Deciding he couldn't draw, they demoted him to a beginner's level. That didn't matter to van Gogh, because he was there for the models, not the instructors. He said he learned more from the other students than from his professors.

Along with live models, the students used props to practice drawing and painting. One prop was a human

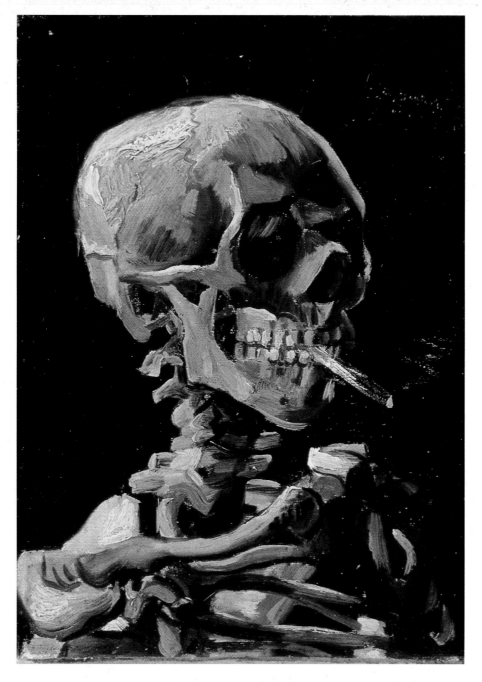

VINCENT VAN GOGH

Skull with Cigarette, 1885

skeleton. Van Gogh masterfully painted the figure, capturing its head and shoulders. It was like a portrait, but of bones. The assignment was meant to be a serious study. Van Gogh didn't see it that way. To be sarcastic, he gave his model a smoke. It was his way of mocking his teachers and their academic, old-fashioned way of thinking.

Although the school was free, Antwerp was an expensive city to live in. Van Gogh hoped to make money by selling drawings and painting portraits but had no success. Theo's monthly payment didn't go far, and Vincent preferred to spend his money on painting materials instead of food. Soon it affected his health. Because of his poor diet, he had stomach pains. His teeth became loose, and eventually several fell out.

After four months in Antwerp, van Gogh was ready to leave. In letter after letter, he pressured Theo about joining him in Paris. Theo tried to put him off, saying he needed time to find a bigger apartment for them to share. In Nuenen, their mother needed help moving to a new home, and Theo suggested that his brother go there to help. Van Gogh wouldn't hear of it. With what little money he had left, he purchased a train ticket to Paris.

VINCENT VAN GOGH

Fishing in Spring, the Pont de Clichy (Asnières), 1887

3 Paris!

PARIS WAS THE ART CENTER of the world, and Theo van Gogh was a rising star. After working for Goupil & Cie. for 13 years, he became the manager of their gallery at 19 Boulevard Montmartre. Located in a fashionable part of town, the gallery had many dedicated customers. Theo earned a good salary and received a commission every time he sold a painting. He was happy to share his earnings with his brother Vincent. Someday he hoped to sell a "van Gogh."

The gallery where Theo worked specialized in the traditional style of painting that had been fashionable in France for hundreds of years. The best paintings, in his bosses' opinion, were done on large canvases using subdued colors and well-blended brush strokes. Theo was successful in selling these types of paintings, but his taste was very different.

Theo liked the painting style of a group of artists called Impressionists. Characterized by colorful, bold brush strokes and depicting modern scenes, the Impressionists' paintings were just becoming popular with art collectors. Until recently, the works had been considered too unconventional for most buyers' tastes. Many people thought the canvases looked messy and unfinished. Theo was one of a small group of art dealers who disagreed. Because Theo was such a good salesman, the owners of Goupil & Cie. allowed him a small space at the gallery to show work by the Impressionists. He promoted their work to anyone who would listen, and his hard work was starting to pay off.

Theo was content with his life. His nice, although small, apartment was a 10-minute walk from the gallery. After work, he could stroll over to cafés to meet his friends.

But one thing troubled him. For several weeks, Vincent had been pestering him about moving to Paris. In his last 15 letters he mentioned it 40 times! Theo loved his brother and wanted to support him. But to actually live with him? He knew Vincent's personality all too well. Like a seesaw, he tipped between being either overly exuberant or ornery and intolerant. Either way, Vincent was a ticking bomb waiting to explode. Helping him from a distance was one thing; having him mess up Theo's apartment and quarrel with his friends was quite another.

First, Theo tried to ignore his brother's hints about coming. When that didn't work, he tried making other suggestions. Theo didn't want to hurt his brother's feelings, but he knew his apartment was too small for them to live together peacefully. When nothing else worked, Theo urged him to at least wait until July. But Vincent had other ideas.

On the first day of March, Theo received another letter. This one wasn't delivered by the postman. Written in black chalk on a scrap of paper torn from a sketchbook, it was hand delivered by a messenger. It said, "My dear Theo, Don't be angry with me for arriving out of the blue. I have thought about it so much, and I believe that in this way we shall save time. . . . We'll fix things up, you'll see. . . . I'll be in the Louvre." In his typically impulsive way, van Gogh had taken the night train from Antwerp, leaving behind a stack of unpaid bills.

Vincent didn't go directly to see his brother. Perhaps he avoided Theo's gallery fearing he'd run into one of his old bosses. Or maybe he realized that barging in at his brother's elegant workplace dressed in tattered clothes wouldn't be the best way to start off. Whatever his reasons, van Gogh sent the message from the train station, then settled into a gallery at the Louvre to wait. Theo felt he had little choice but to take his brother in.

THE PARIS ART SCENE

Van Gogh had come to Paris to pursue painting, and he quickly got down to business. Early each morning, he walked from the apartment he shared with Theo to Fernand Cormon's art studio. Cormon was a successful artist who painted in the style that had been popular for years. His brushstrokes were so well blended that his paintings could be mistaken for a photograph. His large canvases of historical battles were traditional, too.

In addition to painting his own works, Cormon taught a figure-drawing class at his studio. The fact that Cormon's style was different from van Gogh's didn't stop him from enrolling in the class. Cormon knew a lot about drawing the human figure, and he was a tolerant man. Many of his students wanted to paint in new styles, and Cormon didn't restrict them. Because of this, the class was very popular.

Each day, van Gogh spent four hours at Cormon's studio. He sketched figure after figure until he got it right. One student remembered that he would stay long after the rest of the class had left, erasing with such intensity that he wore holes in his drawing paper.

Cormon was a little man with sharp features and a pointy beard. His movements were quick and jerky like a bird's. During class, he stood on a ladder at the front of the room, working on one of his large paintings. Meanwhile, his students sat at their easels at the other end of the studio sketching a model. Most of the students were younger than van Gogh, and they liked to horse around and play tricks on each other. New students were teased the worst. Even though he was the newest student, van Gogh was left alone. The others could sense that the serious Dutchman wasn't one to appreciate a joke, especially if it was on him.

The group was just as lively when discussing art. In those talks, van Gogh always joined in. When he got excited about an idea, van Gogh was an incredible sight, almost frothing at the mouth and trembling with emotion. One student, A. S. Hartrick, remembered him. "He had an extraordinary way of pouring out sentences if he got started, in Dutch, English, and French, then glancing back at you over his shoulder and hissing through his teeth." Hartrick thought many students tolerated van Gogh only because his brother was an art dealer who might someday buy their paintings. Perhaps that was true, but van Gogh also made some very good friends. Two of them were Émile Bernard and Henri de Toulouse-Lautrec.

Each day, after studying at Cormon's, van Gogh went to the Louvre to copy the old masters. He diligently made sketches of their work. He especially respected the work of a fellow Dutchman, Rembrandt van Rijn, who had lived more than 200 years earlier. Van Gogh admired Rembrandt's many self-portraits.

Van Gogh drew at every opportunity. He drew on scraps of paper, letters, books—whatever was at hand when he felt inspired. While sitting at a café, he didn't hesitate to use the border of his menu to sketch the scene he saw from his table.

Van Gogh also studied the work of living artists. Paris was the ideal place to see the latest trends. Because Theo was an art dealer, van Gogh was admitted to all the art exhibitions in town. In 1886 there were four large exhibitions, and van Gogh saw all types of paintings. In May, the Salon held its huge exhibit of the best traditional-style paintings. The Salon had held exhibitions for more than 100 years and was world famous. Cormon's work could be seen there. One month later, the Impressionists held their eighth (and last) exhibition. Paintings using little dots, which were done in a style called Pointillism, made their debut in that exhibition. The work of two Impressionists, Claude Monet and Pierre-Auguste Renoir, could be seen at yet another show, the fifth International Exhibition. Their canvases, filled with bright colors and bold brush strokes, were stunning. Finally, in August, the Salon des Indépendants was held. This exhibition featured artists who chose a variety of styles and broke away from tradition.

Van Gogh was overwhelmed. Theo had written to him about the new styles of painting, but he couldn't

THE IMPRESSIONISTS

CLAUDE MONET

Cliff Walk at Pourville, 1882

TWELVE YEARS BEFORE van Gogh's 1886 arrival in Paris, an art exhibit opened that featured some of the most beautiful, well-loved paintings in the world. Well loved today, that is. In 1874, the artists couldn't even give their work away. The problem was simple: their paintings were different from what people were used to. They preferred works that were painted in a style that had been used for hundreds of years. The best pieces, in their opinion, were done on large canvases, using subdued colors and well-blended brush strokes. They liked noble scenes taken from history—a famous battle, perhaps.

The paintings in the exhibit couldn't have been more different. They were small canvases, filled with quick, loose, brightly colored brush strokes. The subjects were everyday scenes, like a family enjoying a day at the beach. One painting, by a young artist named Claude Monet, was of a harbor scene at sunrise. It especially outraged one critic, Louis Leroy. Its title was *Impression, Sunrise.* When Leroy wrote a review about the event, he jokingly called the group artists in the exhibition "Impressionists." It wasn't meant to be a compliment.

While in Paris, van Gogh met many of the Impressionist artists. One of them, Camille Pissarro, became a good friend.

imagine how dazzling the paintings would be. Inspired, he began using the new ideas in his own work. The muted, gray colors he had used in *The Potato Eaters* were a thing of the past. His new works exploded with brilliant blues, yellows, and oranges. He experimented with different ways of applying the paint, too.

Van Gogh studied at Cormon's art school for three months. Not surprisingly, Cormon's style eventually irritated van Gogh, so he quit and turned to other artists for inspiration.

LIFE WITH THEO

Paris suited van Gogh immensely, and his art progressed as he had hoped. Under Theo's supervision, his health improved, too. His remaining bad teeth were extracted and replaced with a dental plate. He saw Theo's doctor and was treated for the pains that had plagued him in Antwerp.

But as van Gogh's health improved, Theo's got worse. His constitution was weak, and he was frequently ill. Van Gogh's arrival didn't help matters. Sharing a small apartment and experiencing his brother's extreme moods and rude comments wore him down. Theo's good friend, Andries Bonger, referred to his state as "serious problems with his nerves." When Theo came home from work at night, he braced himself for van Gogh's excesses. He was either overly enthusiastic or throwing a tirade. If Theo tried to escape to his room, his brother would follow him, pull up a chair, and

continue for hours. It affected Theo's social life, too. As he predicted, his friends started to avoid visiting him at home. In a letter to his sister Wil, he summed it up. "No one wants to come and see me any more because it always ends in quarrels, and besides, he is so untidy that the room looks far from attractive," he wrote.

The situation improved a bit in June, when Theo found a larger, more expensive apartment. It was located in a section of Paris called Montmartre, near many artists' studios. Situated at the edge of the city, Montmartre was covered in parts with vegetable gardens and a few old windmills. The area closest to their apartment was very lively. It had a local market and many shops. The brothers' fourth-floor apartment was on a hill and had a fantastic view of Paris. Their large living room had a fireplace, and each brother had his own bedroom. Van Gogh turned the largest room in the apartment into a studio. When they hung pictures to decorate the apartment, *The Potato Eaters* was placed in the prized spot.

COLORFUL DISCOVERIES

Quitting Cormon's art class meant van Gogh was on his own. Now that he didn't have live models to draw, he turned to the one model who was always available: himself. While in Paris, he painted at least 28 self-portraits. His first one shows him dressed as a dignified Parisian, in a hat probably borrowed from Theo. The colors and brushwork resemble the darker style of painting he had practiced in Holland.

GEORGES SEURAT

Study for Le Chahut, 1889

Over the next two years, in portrait after portrait, van Gogh experimented with various color combinations and different ways of applying paint. He put away his somber palette of dark green, brown, and gray and started using much brighter colors. Inspired by the Impressionists, he experimented with primary colors: red, yellow, and blue. He combined them with secondary colors: purple, green, and orange. Van Gogh was especially excited about using two colors, called "complementary colors," next to each other. Complementary colors are sometimes called "opposites" because they are directly across from each other on the color wheel. Blue and orange, red and green, and yellow and purple are complementary colors. Van Gogh knew that if he used complementary colors, his picture would seem to vibrate with energy.

Before working with paint, van Gogh experimented with color combinations using strands of yarn. To see how colors looked next to each other, he twisted strands of two colors together and rolled them into a ball. If he liked what he saw, he used the colors in a picture.

Van Gogh also experimented with different types of brush strokes. A new technique called Pointillism was being used by a group of artists known as Neo-Impressionists. Georges Seurat and Paul Signac were two artists who painted in this style. They filled their canvases with dots of paint, thinking the individual dabs of color would blend together when viewed from a distance. A blue dot next to a red dot would blend together and look like purple. Van Gogh tried it in some of his

34

paintings. He didn't have the patience to fill an entire canvas with tiny dots, so he made large splotches of color. His painting *Self-Portrait* was done this way. It's very different from the first self-portrait he painted in Paris. The dash-filled canvas seems to be charged with energy. His choice of colors was important, too. His red beard stands out against the green background because red and green are complementary colors.

As van Gogh had hoped, Paris was a great place to meet other artists. It was an exciting time to be there, too. The city was a thriving, modern place to live and work. Cafés and restaurants lined the avenues, which had sidewalks so wide that chairs and tables could be set up outdoors.

Vincent and Theo frequented the cafés near their apartment in Montmartre. At midday and in the evening, they met at Mother Bataille's restaurant, a cramped but fashionable place where artists, cabaret singers, and writers crossed paths with prominent politicians.

Another restaurant van Gogh liked was called Café du Tambourin. The café had an interesting decor. Tambourines decorated with pictures and poems written by patrons hung on the walls. The stools and tabletops were painted to look like tambourines, too. It was one of van Gogh's favorite hangouts. He ate there often and would pay his bills with paintings, sometimes two or three times a week. Many of the paintings were of flowers. It's thought that van Gogh had a short love affair with the owner, Agostina Segatori. As his friend

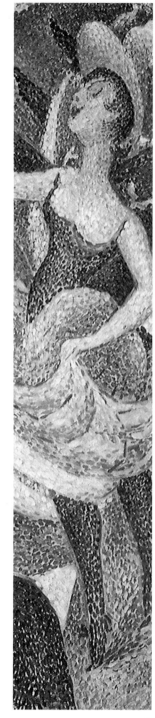

Émile Bernard liked to say, "Instead of real flowers, van Gogh presented her with painted bouquets." Van Gogh painted her, too. In one portrait, she is seated in her café, and Japanese prints hang on the wall behind her.

Van Gogh hung an exhibition of his Japanese prints at the café. The show came to a dramatic head when van Gogh got into an argument with the café's manager. Apparently the manager also had a crush on Segatori. Their quarrel resulted in van Gogh being thrown out of the café. When he returned for his artwork a few months later, he found that the restaurant had gone out of business. He had to fight to get his prints back. Eventually he retrieved most of them and carted them home in a wheelbarrow.

PÈRE TANGUY

One place van Gogh always got a warm welcome was Père Tanguy's art supply store. Tanguy was a good friend to many artists. His little shop was a place for painters like Monet and Renoir to meet. Van Gogh looked forward to seeing whom he'd run into there. Tanguy was a gentle man who enthusiastically supported the young artists. He believed they were geniuses who would soon achieve great success. He helped those who couldn't pay him by trading art supplies for their finished paintings. When Tanguy acquired a new canvas, he placed it in his shop window for everyone to enjoy. Other artists left their work with him as well, hoping he could sell it. Tanguy's collection attracted a lot of interest from everyone who stopped in.

VINCENT VAN GOGH

Self-Portrait, 1887

Artists looked through his shop as if it were a museum. In this way, each one knew what the others were doing.

Van Gogh traded several of his paintings for supplies. Shortly after van Gogh's death, Tanguy sold one of them to an art critic. He charged exactly 42 francs for the piece. When asked how he came up with the price, Tanguy replied, "I looked up what poor van Gogh owed me when he died. It was forty-two francs. Now I have got it back."

There was one painting that Tanguy would never have given up—a portrait of himself. In it, the little shopkeeper is shown against a wall covered with Japanese prints. Van Gogh portrayed him as the gentle man he was. His tightly clasped workman's hands and serene face reflect van Gogh's love for him. Traditionally, portraits were painted with a neutral background, but Van Gogh did the opposite. The Japanese prints jump out from the background with their bright colors and sharp images. Tanguy was very pleased with the painting. When anyone asked him what he would sell it for, he replied, "Five hundred francs." When it was suggested that this was a very high price, he would answer, "I really don't want to sell my portrait at all."

One of the artists van Gogh met at Tanguy's shop was Paul Signac, a painter of dots. Signac understood the color theory that Pointillism was based on and discussed it for hours with van Gogh. He didn't mind van Gogh's excessive manner and noisy company and allowed him to join him while painting. They often hiked to the outskirts of Paris to paint the landscape. Signac described how they

Portrait à la Tanguy

When van Gogh painted a portrait of his favorite shopkeeper, he filled the background with his favorite images. His Japanese prints stand out so much that at first glance, it's hard to see Tanguy! There are scenes of blossoming trees, snow-covered mountain peaks, and women in colorful kimonos. Van Gogh loved the prints and the scenes they depicted.

What images would you include in a background made up of your favorite things? Make a collage of them, and add a portrait of someone special.

MATERIALS

Old magazines

Scissors

2 sheets 11-by-14-inch drawing paper

Glue stick

Pencil

Painting supplies, pastels, or colored pencils

1. Pull out pages from magazines that have pictures of things that you like. They could be favorite foods, places, activities, or animals. The pictures should be at least 3 by 3 inches large. Choose at least 10—you may not use them all.

2. Cut the pictures out in square or rectangular shapes.

3. Arrange your pictures on a piece of drawing paper, filling the entire piece. If an image is too large, you can trim it (around the ears of a cat, for example) and overlap it onto the neighboring picture. Glue the pieces in place.

4. On a separate sheet of paper, draw a portrait of a friend. Include the top of the subject's head down to his or her knees. The portrait should take up about ¾ of the paper.

5. Add color to your portrait and cut it out, closely following its shape.

6. Glue the portrait onto your collage in the same spot van Gogh placed Tanguy: centered, with its bottom edge at the bottom of the collage.

VINCENT VAN GOGH

Le Père Tanguy, 1887

37

JAPANESE PRINTS

IN THE 1600S, Japanese artists developed a style of printmaking called Ukiyo-e, which means "image of the floating world." The prints depicted scenes from everyday life and the interests of ordinary people, such as flowering fruit trees, snow-covered mountains, and women dressed in colorful kimonos. The one shown here by Sharaku is of a popular Kabuki actor.

In the 1800s, Japanese prints were exported all over the world, and Westerners were fascinated by them. They were all the rage in Paris.

To make an Ukiyo-e print, an artist painted a picture on paper. Next, a craftsman carved this image into the surface of a block of wood. A separate block was carved for each color in the image. To make a print, they inked the wood and pressed it onto a sheet of paper. Each color was printed, one at a time, on top of the previous one. Western artists admired the flat, pure colors. They collected the inexpensive prints and many, like van Gogh, were influenced by them.

TŌSHŪSAI SHARAKU

Nakayama Tomisaburō as Miyagino, 1794

went to paint at the village of Asnières one day. Van Gogh argued the whole way home, gesturing this way and that with his large, freshly painted canvas. By the time they arrived, he had splattered himself and everyone he passed with streaks of wet paint. It wasn't unusual for van Gogh to be covered with dabs of paint. Someone once called him a walking example of Pointillism.

Van Gogh also painted with his old classmate Émile Bernard. At 18, the slender, dark-haired artist was 15 years younger than van Gogh, now 33. Bernard still lived with his parents in Asnières, and his father wasn't pleased that he wanted to be an artist. One day, van Gogh met Bernard's father. When van Gogh told him he should be more supportive of his son's career, they got into a terrible argument.

Van Gogh thought Bernard had great talent. He was right—Bernard went on to become a successful artist. He was also a diligent letter writer. After van Gogh left Paris, he and Bernard kept in touch by mail. In their letters they discussed what they were working on as naturally as if they were sitting together at a café.

Theo introduced his brother to several artists, too. Camille Pissarro, an older gentleman, was one of the original Impressionist painters. He helped many of the younger ones, giving them advice about painting as well as being a true friend.

Paul Gauguin was another artist van Gogh met through Theo. Like van Gogh, Gauguin started his career as an artist late in life. Van Gogh was impressed by the quality of Gauguin's work and urged Theo to buy some of his pieces. Gauguin's paintings were colorful, and so was he. The van Gogh brothers spent many nights listening to Gauguin's tales of traveling and painting in far-off lands.

Perhaps van Gogh's most flamboyant friend was Henri de Toulouse-Lautrec. Lautrec stood only 4 feet 11 inches tall, but his personality was larger than life. He came from a wealthy family of French nobility but felt most comfortable among cabaret performers and the seamy side of life. Lautrec became a brilliant poster artist. His images of cabaret performers were created using flat planes of color. They resembled Japanese prints.

Lautrec's favorite place to sketch was the Moulin Rouge, a rowdy gathering spot where patrons drank absinthe while watching dancers perform the cancan. Absinthe was a popular green-colored liqueur. It was so strong it was thought to make people insane. Eventually the toxic drink was banned in France. At times van Gogh joined Lautrec in visiting the cabarets around Montmartre and drinking absinthe.

Toulouse-Lautrec loved to have a good time. Every Sunday he invited artists and critics to gather at his studio to socialize. Van Gogh saw the gatherings as an opportunity to display his work. Week after week he showed up carting one of his paintings. He'd stand it in the corner where it would get good light and then wait for someone to notice it. Sitting opposite his picture, he watched the others as they glanced at his work.

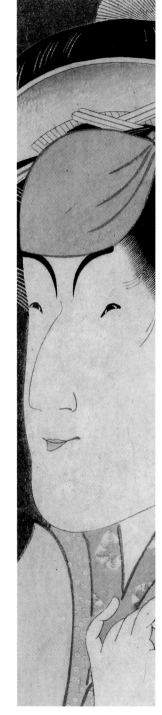

IMPERIAL CROWN FRITILLARIA

VINCENT VAN GOGH

Imperial Crown Fritillaria in a Copper Vase, 1887

UNLIKE SOME OF HIS artist friends, van Gogh was open-minded about trying a variety of painting techniques. Sometimes he used several techniques in one picture. His painting *Imperial Crown Fritillaria* is a perfect example. Van Gogh used the dots of Pointillism for the background but the bold brushstrokes of Impressionism for the flowers and vase. He also applied what he knew about color theory. The orange flowers jump out from the blue background because the colors are complementary.

The signature in the upper left corner of *Fritillaria* simply says "Vincent." In Paris and afterward, van Gogh used only his first name when he signed a painting. There are two reasons why. For Frenchmen, the name "van Gogh" is almost impossible to pronounce. In Dutch, it's pronounced "van hhhock," and the French have difficulty pronouncing the letter *h*. "Vincent," however, was easy to say. Another reason is that Vincent may also have wanted to distance himself from the van Gogh name. He was very different from the long line of conservative van Goghs who came before him. He saw himself as an individual, and using his first name allowed him to be unique.

Van Gogh didn't sign all his work. Of nearly 900 paintings, he only signed 130. Signing his painting was his way of saying "I think this one is really good."

He quietly waited for someone to comment, but they never did.

Van Gogh was very ambitious about having his work seen. While in Paris, he arranged an exhibition of his paintings, along with those of other artists he admired. His intention was to bring together all his new artist friends. The exhibition, held at the Restaurant du Chalet, featured 150 works. Bernard and Gauguin exhibited several pieces. But to van Gogh's disappointment, his friends Seurat, Signac, and even Pissarro refused to participate. Because Bernard and Gauguin didn't hide the fact that they hated Pointillism, the two groups did not get along. Van Gogh's exhibition was visited by a number of artists and dealers. Bernard sold his first painting there. The exhibition was a success but didn't accomplish what van Gogh had intended. Finally, he even took his paintings out of the show. After an argument with the owner of the restaurant, van Gogh joined Seurat and Signac at a different exhibition.

READY FOR A CHANGE

Life in Paris didn't turn out to be all that van Gogh had dreamed. So many of his efforts turned out badly that he began to loathe Paris. Even though he had some friends among the artists, his bad temper caused one unpleasant scene after another. Big cities had never been the best place for him. He became increasingly restless, thinking he needed an entirely new setting to work in.

A few months earlier, Gauguin had returned from Martinique, an island in the Caribbean. Van Gogh spent many evenings listening to his stories about painting in the tropical paradise.

He was ready for a change. In the two years he had lived in Paris, he had learned about color and met many talented artists. Now it was time to move on. Attracted by the idea of warm, sunny landscapes and small, quaint villages, van Gogh decided to go to the south of France.

The sunny south, he thought, would resemble Japan! Van Gogh imagined blossoming fruit trees, pure blue skies, and a landscape filled with large areas of bright color. There were mountain peaks too—just like those in his Japanese prints.

Before leaving, van Gogh asked Bernard to come to the apartment he shared with Theo. They arranged van Gogh's room to give the impression that he was still there. They put up new Japanese prints, leaned a painted canvas against an easel, and placed others against the wall—just as van Gogh would often do when he was there. In this way, Theo would still have him as a companion when he came home, if only in spirit. When they finished, van Gogh embraced Bernard and made him promise to visit him in the south.

Van Gogh's leaving brought the two brothers back together again. They celebrated his last day in Paris by going to a concert. Then they walked over to Georges Seurat's studio to see what he was working on. On February 19, 1888, van Gogh boarded a train for Arles, France.

In Arles, van Gogh would paint the greatest pictures of his career. But his time there would also take a toll.

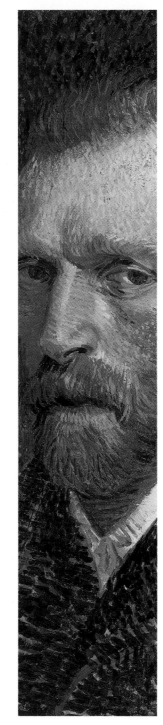

Japanese Fold-Out Album

Van Gogh wanted his drawings made into fold-out albums that he could give to his friends. Make your own album of small sketches. Display it standing on edge, or turn its pages to reveal each drawing one at a time.

My dear Theo,

You know what you must do with these drawings—make sketchbooks with 6 or 10 or 12 like those books of original Japanese drawings. I very much want to make such a book for Gauguin, and one for Bernard.

Ever yours, Vincent

— Letter from Vincent van Gogh to Theo van Gogh (excerpt), Arles, May 28, 1888

1. First, create your artwork. Draw 2 lines to divide a piece of paper into 4 sections that measure 5 ½ by 4 ¼ inches each. Repeat on second piece of paper.

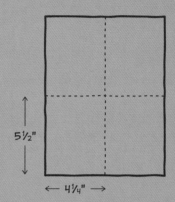

MATERIALS

4 sheets of 8 ½-by-11-inch white paper
Pencil
Ruler
Drawing materials
Scissors
Clear tape
Glue stick

2. Place your paper horizontally and make a drawing in each section. On the second piece of paper, make 3 drawings. In the last section, design a cover for your album.

COVER

3. Cut the 7 drawings and 1 cover out and set them aside.

4. Make your album by cutting a sheet of blank paper in half to make 2 pieces that measure 4 1/4 by 11 inches each. Repeat with a second sheet of paper.

5. Place the pieces end to end and tape them together to make one 44-inch-long strip.

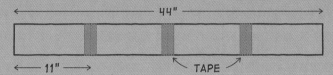

6. Starting at one end, fold the strip over 5 1/2 inches to the taped joint. Turn the strip over and fold 5 1/2 inches again. Continue turning and folding, accordion-style, until the strip is a 5 1/2-by-4 1/4-inch booklet.

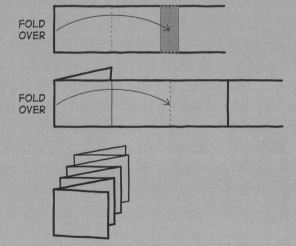

7. Place the booklet so that its topmost folded edge is on the right. This is the cover.

8. Apply glue stick to the back of your cover design, and adhere it to the cover of the booklet.

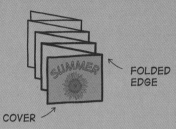

9. Pull the cover to the left, opening the booklet.

10. Decide where you want to place each drawing, and glue each in position.

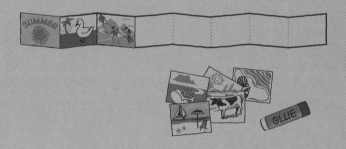

11. To view your album, either fold it into a booklet and turn each page, or place it standing up on its edge in a long zigzag.

VINCENT VAN GOGH

Drawbridge at Arles with a Group of Washerwomen
(Pont de Langlois, Arles, France), 1888

44

VAN GOGH ARRIVED in Arles the following day after a 16-hour journey. As his train approached the station, he opened the carriage window and stuck out his head to take in the view. He expected to see a landscape of dazzling colors drenched in sunshine. To his surprise, the countryside was blanketed in two feet of snow, and more was falling. It was nothing like he had imagined.

But when he got off the train and looked into the distance, he was thrilled. Across the plain, the distant mountains were topped with snow. To van Gogh's delight, southern France really could look like a Japanese print.

Why van Gogh chose Arles is unknown. Perhaps Toulouse-Lautrec, who was from the south, had mentioned it. Van Gogh later told a friend he had only planned a short visit in Arles before continuing farther south. But when he got there, he was fascinated. Arles is in a beautiful region of southeastern France called Provence. The village and its surrounding farmland offered unlimited possibilities for a painter. He decided to stay and paint its marvelous scenes.

Van Gogh lugged his baggage through the snowdrifts, passing through the ancient gates of the town. He didn't have to go far before finding a room at the Hôtel Carrel. Although the rent was higher than he had anticipated, his room was large—big enough for him to set up his easel and work indoors until the weather warmed up. Located on the upper floor, it had a marvelous view of the rooftops of Arles.

The cold weather didn't dampen van Gogh's enthusiasm. He was full of ideas about what to paint, and he started immediately. Looking out his hotel window, he

Sunny Springtime Bird Feeder

When the weather warms up, the world springs to life, drawing out both artists and animals alike. Birds will love this van Gogh–inspired treat. Have your sketchpad ready when they come to visit.

MATERIALS

¼ cup sunflower seeds

Plate

Bagel

Butter knife

Peanut butter

9-by-12-inch piece of yellow craft foam

Scissors

Toothpicks

Chopstick or 8-inch twig

Yarn

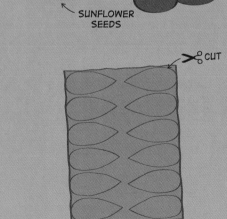

SUNFLOWER SEEDS

PEANUT BUTTER

1. Pour the sunflower seeds onto a plate.

2. Slice a bagel in half and set one half aside.

3. Spread peanut butter onto the cut side of the bagel.

4. Press the bagel into the plate of seeds so that they stick into the peanut butter.

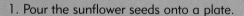 CUT

5. Cut 12 petal shapes about 4 inches long from the foam.

6. Fold the bottom of one petal over ½ inch and gently push a toothpick through the 2 layers of foam. Unfold the foam and position it on the toothpick so that the petal covers only ½ the length of the pick.

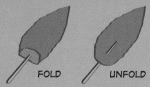

FOLD   UNFOLD

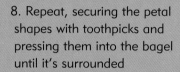

7. Poke the bare end of the toothpick into the side of the bagel.

8. Repeat, securing the petal shapes with toothpicks and pressing them into the bagel until it's surrounded

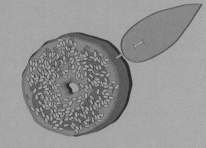

9. Poke a chopstick or twig through the bagel below its hole. This is a perch for the birds.

10. Thread a 2-foot length of yarn through the center of the bagel. Secure the ends and hang your sunflower treat outside.

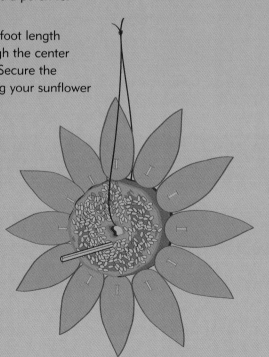

painted the storefront of the butcher shop across the street. One day he bundled up and went outdoors to snip a branch from an almond tree that was full of buds. He painted the branch after it burst into bloom in his warm room a few days later. Eagerly he waited for spring to arrive. He knew the countryside was covered with entire orchards ready to blossom.

Three weeks after van Gogh's arrival, the weather warmed up and he ventured out, equipped to paint. His outdoor painting gear included a portable easel and a box filled with tubes of paint, brushes, turpentine, and other miscellaneous items. He strapped his equipment to his back and, when fully loaded, thought he looked like a bristling porcupine. He wore a blue workman's jacket and pants, topped with a type of floppy straw hat worn by the local shepherds. His clothes were covered with colorful dabs of paint from wiping off brushes and carrying wet canvases.

On the outskirts of town, van Gogh discovered a little drawbridge spanning a canal. The canal was used to irrigate the surrounding farmland, but the ladies of Arles had another use for its sparkling blue water. Along the banks of the canal he spotted a group of women wearing colorful smocks washing their laundry. This was just the type of scene that appealed to van Gogh. He set up his easel to capture it, adding a little horse-drawn wagon on the bridge. Van Gogh liked the drawbridge so much he painted it many times. He made five oil paintings, a watercolor, and two pen-and-ink drawings of it.

Almost every afternoon he wrote to Theo to tell him about his work. Writing about the drawbridge, he carefully described the colors he used. "It is a drawbridge with a little cart going over it, outlined against a blue sky—the river blue as well, the banks orange with green grass." While in Arles, van Gogh also wrote to several of his artist friends, often adding little sketches to illustrate his ideas.

In April, he wrote that he was in "a frenzy of work." As he predicted, the orchards had burst into a sea of blossoms. There were almond trees, cherries, peaches, plums, apricots, pears, and apples. Van Gogh was dazzled by the trees' pink and white blossoms shimmering against the brilliant blue sky. Worried that the petals would start to drop off, he painted feverishly. He could work incredibly fast. Years earlier in art school, Bernard remembered, van Gogh could complete three paintings of a model while the other students had only finished her foot. In Arles, he painted 14 orchards in one month and used up more than 100 tubes of color. Then, worried that Theo wouldn't send him extra money to buy more paint, he made a dozen drawings in pen and ink.

Although the icy weather had passed, painting outdoors could still be unpleasant. A seasonal wind called the mistral was so strong, local folklore claimed it drove people insane. On days when he was up to the challenge, van Gogh set his easel up outside and fastened it to the ground with pegs. When the gales were too strong for that, he laid his canvas on the ground and painted on his knees.

PAUL CÉZANNE

PAUL CÉZANNE

Houses in Provence (Vicinity of L'Estaque), c. 1883

VINCENT VAN GOGH WASN'T the only artist roaming the hills of Provence. Fifty miles to the east in the town of Aix-en-Provence, Paul Cézanne was also painting the landscape. Fourteen years older than van Gogh, he started out exhibiting his work in Paris with Monet and the other original Impressionists. But Paris didn't appeal to him, and he soon moved back home to southern France. He would occasionally return to Paris, but he never stayed long.

Although it would take years before Cézanne won popular acclaim, he was revered by many of the younger artists. Like van Gogh, he exchanged artwork for tubes of paint at Père Tanguy's art supply store. Other artists flocked there to see his work.

One day Cézanne and van Gogh met at Tanguy's. According to Bernard, they did not hit it off. Boldly, van Gogh showed Cézanne his work. "After inspecting everything," Bernard remembered, "Cézanne, who was a timid but violent person, told him, 'Honestly, your painting is that of a madman.'" Van Gogh didn't think much of Cézanne's work, either. He thought the older artist's brushstrokes were "almost timid."

Cézanne's technique was quite different from van Gogh's. His paintings seem to be made up of many rectangular patches of color. Using only a few hues, he applied his paint with great care, slowly laying down one brushstroke at a time. Because his style is so different from the Impressionists, he became known as a Post-Impressionist.

After his death in 1906, Cézanne's reputation grew with astounding speed. His style of painting influenced the next generation and paved the way for the Cubists and Fauves. Today, Cézanne is called the father of Modern Art.

A STRANGER

Arles met all of van Gogh's artistic expectations. Even with its harsh weather, the bright colors of the south were exactly what he had hoped for. The landscape was full of farms, vineyards, and vistas. He especially liked the flat plain around Arles. It was similar to the Netherlands and made him feel at home. Still, something was missing.

In Paris he could see someone he knew just by walking down the street. Now he was alone. Sometimes he went for days without speaking to anyone. He did make a few friends in Arles, but on the whole the villagers thought he was odd. Most of them kept their distance. Not used to seeing artists wandering the countryside, they were suspicious of him. He dressed in his paint-stained clothes and floppy straw hat. His habit of stopping and peering at things—which is natural for a painter—made some people wonder if he was crazy.

It wasn't long before teenage boys started making fun of him. They screamed "Fou-rou!"—crazy redhead—as he passed. Van Gogh knew they were calling him names. "Fame at last," he commented in a letter to Theo. Years later, one of the boys, who became a librarian, realized that van Gogh was "really a gentle person, a creature who would probably have liked us to like him, and we left him in his terrifying isolation, the terrible loneliness of genius."

The innkeeper at the Hôtel Carrel treated him badly, too. Because van Gogh painted so many canvases, he began to set some in the hallway outside his room. Seeing a chance to get more rent, the innkeeper decided to charge van Gogh a storage fee. When van Gogh refused to pay it, the man confiscated his artwork. Van Gogh took him to court and won. Then he gathered his canvases and moved out.

Van Gogh no longer needed space at the hotel. While exploring the village, he had found the perfect place to set up his studio. It was a little house painted the color of butter. Van Gogh named it the Yellow House.

THE YELLOW HOUSE

Even before he left Paris, van Gogh dreamed of starting an artists' colony in the south. He imagined a band of brother artists who would live and paint together under the brilliant sun. They would all have their own unique style of painting but share a common goal. Working side by side, they would exchange ideas and comment on each other's work.

At the time, two of the artists he knew from Paris were doing just that. Bernard and Gauguin had gathered with other artists on the western coast of France. They lived in a town called Pont-Aven in the region called Brittany. Gauguin was considered the leader of the group, which was known as the Pont-Aven School.

Van Gogh would have welcomed many of the artists to his "Studio of the South." In a letter to Theo, he wondered about a potential first guest. "Perhaps Gauguin would come south?" he wrote.

VINCENT VAN GOGH

Postman Joseph Roulin, 1888

Van Gogh admitted the Yellow House needed a lot of work before he could invite guests. *He* couldn't even live there. The building had been shut up for a long time and was in poor condition. It didn't have hot water or the gas needed for lighting in 1888. What's more, the bathroom was in a hotel behind the house. Still, it had potential. He found lodgings at a nearby hotel and began to fix it up. For the next four months, while furiously painting new canvases, he had the house repaired.

Using what money he had left from Theo's monthly allowance, he had the house painted. The outside was yellow with vivid green shutters. Inside, he painted the walls white and the doors blue, which looked vibrant against the red tiles on the floor. The fresh coat of paint did wonders for the house, but it still didn't have furniture.

Van Gogh slept at the hotel and worked in the studio he set up on the first floor of the house. He didn't have much privacy while working. The windows in his studio faced the street, and passersby could peer in. But van Gogh didn't mind being watched as he painted. He felt that if people saw him at work they would understand how serious his job was. He enjoyed hearing the murmur of their voices as they passed his window and the clopping of horse hooves on the street.

Now that he had a studio, van Gogh hoped to find models who would pose for him. Painting portraits had always been important to him. He saw it as a way to be in the company of another soul and portraying his or her humanity for future generations. Unfortunately, it wasn't easy to find models. True, his personality made people nervous. Beyond that, some were superstitious about having their likeness taken. In 1888 many people around the world worried that having their image painted or photographed would result in illness or death. The people in Arles were no different. Van Gogh had a hard time convincing them otherwise. But his luck changed when he met a humble postal worker.

In July, van Gogh found—to his delight—a whole family of models. Joseph Roulin and his wife lived near the Yellow House and were the first people in Arles van Gogh could call friends. Roulin was a postal official, but van Gogh referred to him as a postman. He was a kind man, and even though he wasn't quite old enough to be van Gogh's father, that's how Vincent thought of him. He enjoyed Roulin's stories, which he told at the local café over a bottle of wine.

Roulin and his wife, Augustine, invited van Gogh to their home to paint their portraits. He eventually painted the entire family. First, he portrayed the postman in his blue uniform with gold buttons. His cap was lettered "Postes" in bright gold, too. Van Gogh enjoyed Roulin's company so much he painted seven portraits of him. In addition to the Roulin's two sons, he painted Augustine, who was pregnant at the time, and later their baby girl. To thank them for modeling, van Gogh gave them some of the portraits.

Whenever van Gogh came to paint, the Roulins insisted on sharing their simple meal with him. Spending time with the family and having them as friends must have been good for his morale. As time went on, they seemed to feel protective toward him, and he appreciated their concern.

Van Gogh had a few other friends as well. He met a soldier named Paul-Eugène Milliet who was staying in Arles for a few months between assignments. He was a member of a French infantry unit called Zouaves and wore a flamboyant uniform: short blue jacket embellished with swirling red trim, bright blue cummerbund, wild red pantaloons, and matching red stocking cap topped with a tassel. The handsome young soldier didn't like to sit still, but van Gogh managed to paint his portrait. Milliet was interested in art, and van Gogh gave him a few lessons. Most of all, Milliet liked to chase girls. "Milliet probably wouldn't get the girls," van Gogh grumbled to Theo, "if he were an artist."

A few professional artists passed through Arles, too. Eugène Boch, who was from Belgium, spent time with van Gogh during a summer visit. They hiked together, debated about art, and talked about the coal mining district in Belgium where van Gogh once lived. Boch, who was also a poet, had a "face like a razor blade" and a pointy beard. When van Gogh painted Boch's portrait, he added a dreamy, poetic touch. He painted the background of the picture dark blue like the night sky. Behind Boch's pale head, he added shimmering stars.

The night sky in Arles dazzled van Gogh. Its rich, dark blue color, filled with stars, interested him as much

VINCENT VAN GOGH

Café-Terrace at Night (Place du Forum in Arles), 1888

as the sunny orchards filled with blooms. He decided to work outside at night, but first he had to figure out how. The streets of Arles were dark, making it impossible to see what he was doing when he applied paint to his canvas. He solved the problem by sticking candles in a ring around the crumbling brim of his straw hat. When lit, they allowed him to see his canvas.

One evening, he set his easel on the cobblestone street across from a café. He lit his candle-topped hat and painted a masterpiece. The café's yellow terrace, lit with gaslight, glows under a star-filled sky. Van Gogh enjoyed painting "a night picture without any black, nothing but beautiful blue and violet and green."

In September, van Gogh moved into the Yellow House. With extra money he received from Theo, he bought simple things for his bedroom and a more luxurious walnut bed for his guestroom. "I have it all planned," he wrote while sitting in the Café de la Gare. "I really do want to make it—an artist's house. . . . Everything from the chairs to the pictures full of character." The best way to create an artist's house, he thought, would be to decorate the walls with his own paintings.

For the next month, he worked with determination. He painted five large pictures in one week. Completely exhausted, he slept 16 hours in one night. He had, as he put it, a "queer turn," some sort of attack or collapse. Van Gogh feared, not for the first time, that he was going mad. Poor diet was one of the causes of van Gogh's ill health. For days on end, he lived on nothing but bread and coffee. He was also drinking heavily.

THE VISITOR

Anxiety was another reason why van Gogh felt on the verge of a breakdown. His first guest, Paul Gauguin, was due to arrive any day. Ever since he signed the lease for the Yellow House, van Gogh had pressured Theo to arrange a deal with Gauguin: free room and board, including an allowance, in exchange for twelve paintings a year. The one stipulation: he had to live with van Gogh in the Yellow House.

In truth, Gauguin had no desire to stay with van Gogh. On the occasions he met him in Paris, he found him irritating. On the other hand, Theo was in a position to help him quite a bit. Theo had already sold a few of Gauguin's canvases and planned to hold an exhibition of his work. Gauguin was in debt, and Theo's offer was too good to turn down. Moving to Arles allowed him to escape his money worries for a while, in addition to pleasing Theo. It also gave Gauguin a chance to save up to pursue his own dream: to live and paint in Tahiti.

When van Gogh heard that Gauguin agreed to come, he was elated. Frantic to impress his guest, van Gogh said he had "no time to think or feel; I just go on painting like a locomotive." He set about making his guestroom as welcoming as possible. Sunflowers were van Gogh's favorite flower, and Provence was covered with fields of them. He decided to greet Gauguin with a room filled with sunflowers—paintings, of course. He arranged fresh-cut sunflowers in a simple vase and painted six luminous pictures. From these, he chose two to hang in Gauguin's bedroom.

Vincent's Sunflowers

Decorate your own room with a vase filled with fabulous sunflowers. Your work of art will be almost as large as Vincent's 37-by-29-inch masterpiece!

MATERIALS

Picture of *Sunflowers* on page viii (for reference)
Yellow poster board, 28 by 22 inches
Pencil
Glue stick
½ cup ground coffee
Newspaper
Squeezable bottle of white glue, ½–¾ full
Orange poster or acrylic paint
Spoon
Mixing stick
Marker

1. Use a pencil to draw a horizontal line across your poster board about 6 inches from the bottom. Draw a large vase that extends above and below this line.

2. Visualize how your sunflowers will fill the vase and draw their round centers on the poster board.

3. Apply glue stick to one flower center. Sprinkle the ground coffee over the glue, and press it in place. Repeat for all the sunflower centers. Tap the excess coffee onto newspaper.

4. Add about a spoonful of orange paint to the bottle of glue, stir it in, and replace the cap.

5. Squeeze the colored glue onto the poster board using squiggles, dots, and lines to create petals around the flower centers. Decorate the vase and tabletop with the colored glue, too. Let dry overnight.

6. Use a marker to sign your name on the vase as van Gogh did.

He made space in his studio for Gauguin to work and had gas lines put in the main room. They would be able to work into the night by the light of gas lamps. There were no gas lines upstairs in their bedrooms, so they'd have to use candles after dark.

Van Gogh wanted everything to be perfect when Gauguin arrived. As the time came near, he was consumed with anxiety. He feared Gauguin wouldn't like Arles and would be angry with van Gogh for bringing him there. He was so agitated that he feared he would become ill. Perhaps as a way to calm himself, van Gogh decided to paint a picture that would make people think "of rest." It was a picture of his newly decorated bedroom. Painting a picture of his bedroom was also a way to confirm that the Yellow House had become his home.

THE ARRIVAL

Before Gauguin left for Arles, he and van Gogh exchanged self-portraits. It was van Gogh's idea, a way to see each other's recent work. When Gauguin's portrait arrived, van Gogh took it to the Café de la Gare to show all the regulars. He told them to be on the lookout for his guest.

Gauguin arrived just after five o'clock in the morning on October 23, 1888. He walked the short distance from the train station to van Gogh's house but found its shutters closed. Not wanting to disturb his host's sleep, Gauguin went to wait at a nearby café. When he opened the door and stepped inside, the owner looked up and exclaimed, "You're the pal. I recognize you!"

At dawn, Gauguin went to the Yellow House and knocked on the door. It was the first day of a visit that would last nine weeks.

From the beginning, Gauguin wondered whether he had made a mistake in coming. He could see that van Gogh lived a chaotic life. The first sign was his studio. "I was shocked," Gauguin wrote. "His box of colors barely sufficed to contain all those squeezed tubes, which were never closed up." Looking past the mess, he saw a stunning sight. Pictures were everywhere.

The morning sun shone through the studio window and lit up dozens of paintings. They hung on the walls, were stacked in corners, and perched on van Gogh's easel. All of them were done in a style that was uniquely van Gogh's. When he went upstairs, Gauguin was especially taken with the two paintings of sunflowers that decorated his room.

As he settled in, Gauguin began making changes. Seeing that van Gogh could hardly remember to eat, he took over the job of cooking. Van Gogh was also bad at managing money, so Gauguin organized their finances. At the beginning of each month, they pooled their money from Theo in a small box. Whenever they needed cash, to buy groceries for instance, the amount taken out was written on a piece of paper and put in the box. In this way, they kept track of their expenses.

When it came to painting, Gauguin also took charge—appointing himself the master. Gauguin had a large ego, and he was bossy and critical of van Gogh's

Create a "Self-Portrait" of Your Room

Imagine yourself stepping into The Bedroom *and plopping down on one of van Gogh's straw chairs. Looking around, you'd notice things that would tell you something about him. In a way, it's a portrait of van Gogh. See if you can find the items listed below. Then make a picture-portrait of your own room. Include things that tell a viewer something about yourself.*

Can you find these items in van Gogh's room?

❀ Van Gogh's straw hat   ❀ Mirror
❀ Brush   ❀ Painter's smock
❀ 2 portraits   ❀ Towel
❀ Painting of a   ❀ Knob on a drawer
    landscape

Bonus question: Did van Gogh sign his painting?

MATERIALS

Drawing materials such as colored pencils, pastels, or markers
Paper

1. Think about what items in your bedroom say something about who you are.

2. Make a drawing of your room. You don't need to include everything, just the things that give viewers an idea of what is important in your life and the things you are proud of (or maybe not so proud of). Perhaps you'll draw a guitar resting in the corner, a poster of your favorite singer, or a messy dresser piled high with books.

3. Compare your picture with van Gogh's. Do your bedrooms have anything in common?

VINCENT VAN GOGH
The Bedroom, 1889

55

PAUL GAUGUIN

Madame Roulin, 1888

preferred to use thin, flat planes of color and simplified shapes. He worked much slower. Van Gogh thought it was important to work directly from nature. His paintings resembled the actual scenes fairly closely, but he sometimes altered the colors. Gauguin preferred to paint his subjects from memory, using his imagination to modify the scene. This gave his paintings a dreamlike quality.

In fact, the two men were quite different. Van Gogh was thin and frail and moved with disturbingly fast, jerky movements. A writer named Charles Morice described Gauguin as having "heavy eye-lids that opened lazily over slightly bulging, bluish eyes that rotated in their sockets to look to the left and right almost without the body or the head having to take the trouble to move." When Gauguin spoke, his speech was slow and somber. On the other hand, words poured out of van Gogh. At times, he couldn't stop speaking.

Even though they were so different, they seemed to get along—for the first few weeks, anyway. Van Gogh was happy to have company at the Yellow House, and they settled in comfortably.

After painting all day, Gauguin made dinner. "He cooks perfectly," van Gogh wrote to Theo, "I think I shall learn from him." But the one time he tried making soup, even van Gogh had to laugh. "How he mixed it I don't know," Gauguin wrote, "as he mixed his colors in his pictures I dare say. At any rate, we couldn't eat it."

It was van Gogh's job to buy the groceries, which didn't require much of a trip. The house attached to his

ideas. At first, this didn't bother van Gogh. He respected Gauguin's knowledge and admired his work. Proudly, he took Gauguin to his favorite sites. They painted side by side, just as van Gogh had dreamed they would. They painted together at home, too. One evening, Mrs. Roulin came to pose, and both artists painted a portrait of her.

The two artists painted the same scenes, but their styles were very different. They both liked to use bright colors, but van Gogh used vigorous brushstrokes and quickly covered his canvas in thick paint. Gauguin

was used as a small grocery store, literally on the other side of the wall. He only had to step next door.

After dinner, the two artists often went to the Café de la Gare and discussed art over many drinks. There Gauguin met Milliet, Roulin, and other regulars of the café who knew van Gogh.

THE CRISIS

As van Gogh had hoped, the "brotherhood of artists" exchanged ideas. Gauguin encouraged van Gogh to work from his imagination, and van Gogh was open to the suggestion. He wrote to his sister Wil about it. "Gauguin gives me the courage to imagine things, and certainly things from the imagination take on a more mysterious character." After trying it, however, van Gogh decided it wouldn't work for him.

Both artists had strong opinions, and before long, they began having endless arguments. "He likes my paintings very much," Gauguin wrote to Bernard in a letter, "but while I am doing them he always finds that I am doing this or that wrong." Van Gogh told Theo, "Our arguments are terribly electric, sometimes we come out of them with our heads as exhausted as a used electric battery."

Even though they weren't getting along, van Gogh wanted Gauguin to stay. He was worried because they had gotten word from Theo that he had sold some of Gauguin's paintings. Although he was happy for Gauguin, the news made van Gogh miserable. He knew

Gauguin wanted to go to Tahiti. With the sale of his paintings, he could almost pay for his trip.

With his nerves on edge, van Gogh began to act strangely. "During the latter days of my stay," Gauguin wrote, "Vincent would become excessively rough and noisy, and then silent. On several nights I surprised him in the act of getting up and coming over to my bed. . . . It was enough for me to say quite sternly, 'What's the matter with you?' for him to go back to bed without a word and fall into a heavy sleep."

Gauguin also claimed that one night while drinking at the café, van Gogh threw a glass of absinthe at his head and then passed out. Luckily, he missed.

That next day, Gauguin sent a letter off to Theo. He told him about the episode in the café and asked for part of the money from the sale of his paintings. "All things considered I am compelled to return to Paris," he wrote. But then Gauguin changed his mind. He felt guilty about deserting van Gogh and was concerned about how Theo might react. Still, his decision to stay didn't make van Gogh any less anxious.

Two days before Christmas, the artists argued again. When Gauguin threatened to leave Arles, van Gogh became agitated and unruly. Hoping van Gogh would calm down, Gauguin decided to take a walk in the public garden. As he crossed the square, he heard van Gogh's quick, short steps coming from behind, and turned. Van Gogh, Gauguin reported, looked quite mad. "You are silent, but I will also be silent," van Gogh said,

Vincent's Mixed-Up Soup

Van Gogh would love this White Bean Soup from Provence—as long as he didn't try to make it himself! It's seasoned with Herbes de Provence, a mixture of herbs used in dishes from the sunny, hot region of southern France. You'll find it in the spice section of your grocery store.

ADULT SUPERVISION REQUIRED

INGREDIENTS

1 tablespoon extra-virgin olive oil

1 medium-size sweet onion, chopped

½ purple eggplant, peeled and cut into bite-size pieces

1 zucchini, cut into bite-size pieces

2 garlic cloves, chopped

1 (15.5 ounce) can cannellini beans (white kidney beans), drained and lightly rinsed

1 (14.5 ounce) can diced tomatoes

1 tablespoon Herbes de Provence

½ teaspoon salt

1 (14 ounce) can vegetable broth

Salt and pepper to taste

UTENSILS

Knife

Cutting board

Large pot with lid

Large spoon

Can opener

Measuring spoons

Fork

Stovetop

1. Add olive oil to the bottom of a large pot and warm over medium heat for 1 minute.

2. Add onions, eggplant, zucchini, and garlic. Saute for 10 minutes, stirring often, until the onions are soft and transparent.

3. Add the beans, tomatoes, Herbes de Provence, salt, and broth to the pot. If broth doesn't cover vegetables, add water.

4. Turn up the heat so that the soup boils, then lower it to a simmer. Cover and cook for 30 minutes, stirring every 5 minutes. The soup is ready when the eggplant is tender when pierced with a fork.

5. Serve with French bread and butter for a delicious meal.

Serves 4

and ran off. Afraid to sleep in the house that night, Gauguin checked into a hotel and went to bed. Van Gogh returned home.

Later that evening, van Gogh grabbed his shaving razor and cut off part of his left ear. In doing so, he severed an artery, which caused blood to spurt out. He stopped the bleeding using towels, washed the amputated piece, and placed it in an envelope he made from a newspaper. He then put on a beret to cover the injured side of his head and walked to a nearby brothel. He asked for a prostitute he knew named Rachel and handed her the gory package, saying, "Guard this object very carefully." With that, he disappeared down the street.

Somehow van Gogh made it back home. He climbed the blood-spattered stairs to his bedroom, crawled into bed, and fell into a deep sleep. When she discovered what was inside the envelope, Rachel fainted.

The next morning, as Gauguin approached the Yellow House, he knew something was wrong. A large crowd had gathered in the square across from the house. Policemen, alerted by Rachel, stood at the door, about to enter. Looking through the window at the bloody mess, they must have assumed van Gogh was dead. They found him upstairs in bed, rolled up in his sheets—unconscious but still alive.

Gauguin warned the police, "Awaken this man with great care, and if he asks for me, tell him I left for Paris. The sight of me may prove fatal for him." With that, he left to send Theo a telegram. The two artists never saw each other again.

The police were able to wake van Gogh up. He asked for his pipe, his tobacco, and Gauguin. He didn't, or wouldn't, remember the events of the previous night. The police took him to the hospital. They gave his ear, which they had placed in a bottle, to the doctors, but it was too late to sew it back on.

HOPE FOR RECOVERY

When Gauguin's telegram arrived, Theo was sitting in his Paris office in an exceptionally good mood. He had just written to his sister, Elisabeth, telling her of his plans to get married.

Theo had been very lonely after his brother left for Arles. Even though living with him was stressful at times, he "hadn't expected we would become so attached to each other." The apartment seemed empty without him. Ten months after Vincent's departure, Theo fell in love.

His future wife was the sister of his best friend, Andries Bonger. Theo first met Johanna Bonger during a visit with Andries to his family home in Holland. When he was introduced to Andries's youngest sister, Johanna, it was love at first sight—for him. Unfortunately, Jo was in love with someone else. Theo had given up on Jo when, three years later, she came to Paris. She was visiting her brother but was obviously happy to see Theo, too.

Now, just as his happiness with Jo was within reach, Theo received the devastating news from Arles. He sent

A CLOSER LOOK
LA BERCEUSE

VINCENT VAN GOGH

Madame Roulin Rocking the Cradle
(La Berceuse), 1889

AFTER MRS. ROULIN had her baby, van Gogh painted this portrait of her and called it *La Berceuse*, which is French for "The Lullaby." It also means "a woman who rocks an infant," which is exactly what she is doing. Today it's not obvious what the rope in Mrs. Roulin's hand is for. But at the time, everyone looking at the picture would have known. In van Gogh's day, babies slept in small cradles that could be rocked. Instead of leaning down and pushing on it, parents often tied a piece of rope to the cradle. Pulling on the rope made it easy to rock a baby to sleep.

Van Gogh treasured the idea of a mother rocking her baby, but there is a second meaning to his painting. He had recently read a story about fishermen who got homesick during their long journeys. Van Gogh thought that if this picture hung in the sleeping quarters of their boat, when it rocked, they could imagine they were in a rocking cradle. Then they wouldn't be so homesick.

a note to Jo, caught an express train south, and arrived in Arles on Christmas Day.

The doctors told Theo that his brother had lost a lot of blood. However, he would live. "But," Theo wondered, "will he remain insane?" The doctors weren't sure.

Van Gogh had moments when he seemed OK. While Theo visited Vincent at the hospital, Theo talked about his plans to marry and asked if his brother approved. Van Gogh replied yes. He asked for Gauguin "continually," "over and over," Theo reported. But Gauguin refused to visit, claiming it would be too upsetting for van Gogh.

Although lucid at times, Vincent would suddenly start rambling and become overcome with grief. "It was terribly sad being there," Theo wrote to Jo. "From time to time all his grief would well up inside him, and he would try to weep, but couldn't. Poor fighter and poor, poor sufferer. . . . In the next few days they will decide whether he is to be transferred to a special institution."

Heartbroken, Theo returned to Paris, joined by Gauguin. Van Gogh's faithful friend Roulin assumed the responsibility of looking after him. He and his wife took turns visiting him at the hospital. The day after Theo's departure, Roulin thought van Gogh was lost. "Not only is his mind affected, but he is very weak and down-hearted," he wrote to Theo. "When I left him I told him I would come back to see him; he replied we would meet again in heaven."

The next day, Mrs. Roulin paid a visit. "He hid his face when he saw her coming. When she spoke to him, he replied well enough, and talked to her about our little girl and asked if she was still as pretty as ever." When Roulin returned a day later, he learned that after his wife had left, van Gogh suffered a terrible attack. He had to be put in an isolated room, refusing to eat or talk.

After this relapse, to everyone's surprise, van Gogh got better. Within a few days he seemed to be his old self. His doctor Félix Rey, diagnosed van Gogh's problem as seizures triggered by mental stress and poor physical condition. He warned that he would retain his "extreme excitability" because that was his nature.

By Friday, January 4, 1889, he was well enough to leave the hospital for a short visit. He went back to the Yellow House with Roulin by his side. Prior to their visit, Roulin and a housekeeper had scrubbed the blood off the studio floor and stairs and tidied up.

Van Gogh was happy to be back in his studio, surrounded by his paintings. While there, he wrote letters to Theo and Gauguin. "My dear friend Gauguin," he began, "I take the opportunity of my first outing from the hospital to write you a couple of words of my profound and sincere friendship." He then asks Gauguin not to speak ill of "our poor little yellow house."

Two weeks after his breakdown, van Gogh was released from the hospital. Eager to continue working, he finished his portrait of Mrs. Roulin titled *La Berceuse*. He also painted two self-portraits. In them, he wears a

fur cap over his bandaged ear. One painting included two important objects in the background: his easel and a favorite Japanese print.

Within a month, his affliction returned. He imagined that people were trying to poison him and said he heard voices. His cleaning lady, alarmed by his wild outbursts, informed the police. He was readmitted to the hospital, this time for 10 days. When his neighbors heard that he would be released, they were horrified.

Fearing for their safety, 30 neighbors signed a petition claiming van Gogh was dangerous. They said he went around town shouting and grabbing women by the waist. Their petition suggested that he return to live with his family or be sent to an asylum. As a result, the police locked van Gogh in a cell in the hospital, where he spent his days feeling like a caged animal.

A MUCH-NEEDED REST

One day, van Gogh had a visit from an old friend. Paul Signac, the Pointillist painter, was passing through Arles on his way to the Mediterranean coast. He persuaded the authorities to release van Gogh so they could visit the Yellow House for a few hours. The house had been sealed by the police, but Signac forced his way in. When he stepped into the studio, he was amazed. He later wrote about it to a friend. "Imagine the splendor of those white washed walls, in which flowered those colorings in their full freshness." He and van Gogh spent the day looking at his artwork and catching up. "Throughout the day he spoke to me of painting, literature, socialism. In the evening, he was a little tired. There had been a terrific spell of mistral and that may have enervated him. He wanted to drink about a quart of essence of turpentine from the bottle that was standing there. It was high time to return to the asylum."

The next day, the two artists went for a walk. Signac asked van Gogh if he'd like to join him in painting on the Mediterranean coast. Van Gogh declined. He lived in fear of another attack and preferred to spend the next few months in an institution where he could rest and, hopefully, be treated.

Exactly one year after he signed the lease, van Gogh was back at the Yellow House, packing up his pictures. Reverend Frédéric Salles, a Protestant minister in Arles, had helped him find an institution where he could stay. It was 15 miles away in the town of St. Rémy. Instead of setting up a "Studio of the South," he would be entering an institution for the mentally ill.

Draw a Mirror Image

When you look at van Gogh's Self-Portrait with Cut-Off Ear and Bandage, you might think he injured his right ear. The bandage does seem to cover his right ear. Which ear do you think the bandage is covering? If you guessed his left ear, you'd be correct. Van Gogh looked into a mirror when he painted his self-portraits. The painting he made is a mirror image of himself. Try this experiment to see how it works.

MATERIALS

Large mirror

Pencil

Sketchpad

A friend

LEFT ARM

1. Sit in front of a mirror. If you draw with your right hand, hold your left arm out from the

LOOKS LIKE RIGHT ARM

side of your body. If you draw with your left hand, hold out your right arm.

2. While your arm is extended, make a sketch of what you see in the mirror.

3. Show the drawing to a friend and ask him which one of your arms is extended. His answer will be the opposite of what you drew.

VINCENT VAN GOGH

Self-Portrait with Cut-Off Ear and Bandage, 1889

VINCENT VAN GOGH
Stairway at Auvers, 1890

5 The Last Hope

ON MAY 8, 1889, Reverend Salles accompanied van Gogh to the asylum in St. Rémy. At the time, van Gogh was feeling fine and calmly described his symptoms to the director, Dr. Théophile Peyron. The doctor diagnosed his condition as a form of epilepsy. He didn't know what brought on van Gogh's attacks or whether he'd have a relapse. Today there is medication for epilepsy, but in 1889 nothing could be done to ease van Gogh's suffering. It's also likely that he suffered from a combination of problems, including mental illness.

Hoping he'd be there for a short time, van Gogh settled into his new home. At first, he felt positive about the asylum, which was called Saint-Paul-de-Mausole. Because many of the rooms were empty, Theo was able to arrange for his brother to have two rooms. He used the second bedroom as a studio. Van Gogh liked the way his rooms were furnished, but the pretty curtains couldn't change the fact that iron bars covered the windows.

From his bedroom window, van Gogh had a beautiful view of the nearby mountains. His studio overlooked a garden enclosed by a high wall. Although the garden had plenty of weeds, it also overflowed with flowers. In the courtyard, stone benches invited visitors to rest, and a stone fountain sprayed a plume of water into the air.

During the day, van Gogh was free to mingle with the other patients. He soon realized that most of them were much more ill than he was. Sensitive to their suffering, he treated them with kindness. He made a point of chatting with one man who clearly enjoyed his company but could utter only incoherent noises. Ironically, van Gogh felt more comfortable with the patients than

WHAT WOULD DOCTORS SAY TODAY?

BECAUSE VAN GOGH WROTE about his health problems in incredible detail, doctors and researchers have had a field day reviewing his letters. Long after his death, they are still trying to diagnose his illness.

There have been many theories, including brain tumor, glaucoma, manic depression, and absinthe poisoning. Or perhaps digitalis poisoning, which can cause yellow vision. Some suggest that's why van Gogh loved yellow paint.

Another theory is that van Gogh had a disease called acute intermittent porphyria. This condition is often called the royal malady, because it is believed to have afflicted Great Britain's King George III. People suffering from porphyria lack a vital compound in their blood that carries oxygen through their body.

Many of van Gogh's symptoms are consistent with this disease, including his hallucinations, attacks of abdominal pain, depression, and seizures. The symptoms of porphyria are often brought on by exposure to chemicals like those in paints. Poor diet and too much alcohol can also be a factor. Because it is an inherited disease, relatives can be affected. This might explain Theo's poor health, as well as their sister Wil's, who spent half her life in an asylum.

Today, patients can be tested for porphyria and treated. In van Gogh's day, physicians didn't even know about the disease.

he had with many people outside the asylum. After all the years of being an outcast, he was finally accepted for who he was.

Seeing the "madmen and lunatics" in the institution helped him to lose "the vague dread, the fear of the thing." Learning about his illness made it less terrifying. As in the past, he wrote long letters to Theo, expressing his thoughts. "Little by little," he wrote, "I can come to look upon madness as a disease like any other."

He witnessed how epilepsy affected other patients, and it helped him understand his own condition. After a seizure, they would describe what the attack was like. He was surprised that their experiences were similar to his own. They too heard voices and saw distorted shapes.

Van Gogh understood the benefit of a calm, organized routine. Scheduled meals, without alcohol, helped too. He didn't like the food that was served (mostly beans) but filled his plate anyway, hoping he'd recover faster.

In 1889, ideas about both epilepsy and mental illness were very primitive, as were the treatments. Twice a week for two hours at a stretch, van Gogh soaked in a bathtub filled with cold water. This was the only therapy the patients at Saint-Paul-de-Mausole received.

CYPRESSES AND STARRY SKIES

Van Gogh had agreed to enter the asylum with the understanding that he would be allowed to paint. Less than a week after his arrival, he set up his easel in the garden. The other patients were interested in what he was doing but watched from a respectful distance.

VINCENT VAN GOGH

The Starry Night, 1889

67

Make a *Starry Night* Peep Box

Create your own starry night and seal it in a box. Peeking in is like visiting a magical land.

ADULT SUPERVISION REQUIRED

MATERIALS

Shoe box

Scissors

X-Acto knife

Blue poster paint

½-inch-wide paintbrush

Heavyweight drawing paper

Pencil

Ruler

Picture of *The Starry Night* (for reference)

Coloring materials such as paint, markers, or pastels

Clear tape

Wax paper

1. Remove the shoebox lid, and cut out a large rectangle in its center.

2. Cut a peephole in the center of one end of the shoe box. Ask an adult to help.

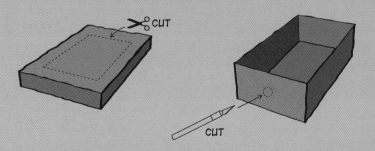

3. Paint the inside of the box and lid's underside blue, and let them dry.

4. Stand the shoebox on its end, on a piece of heavy drawing paper. Trace around it. Remove the shoebox, and add a 1-inch border around the traced shape. Cut out the entire shape, including the border.

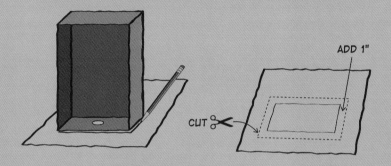

ADD 1"

CUT

5. Repeat step 4 two more times for a total of 3 pieces.

6. Look at van Gogh's painting *The Starry Night*. Think of the picture as having three parts: the starry sky, the village, and the large tree.

7. On one piece of cut paper, paint a starry sky. Fill the entire area inside the border. Note: the 1-inch border will not show and does not need to be painted.

8. On the second sheet of paper, paint your idea of a village. It might be a street of houses, a cityscape, or one house with picket fence. Fill the entire width of paper, inside the border, but only the bottom half to three-fourths of it. Cut around the top edge of your drawing and straight across the side borders where your picture ends.

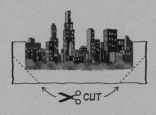
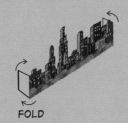
FOLD

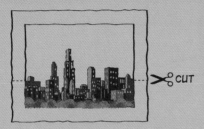
CUT

9. On the remaining sheet of paper, paint a tree. Its top branches should reach the top of the paper but keep inside the border. Add bushes on each side of the tree, filling the entire width of the paper but only the bottom fourth of the piece. Cut around the top edge of your drawing and straight across the side borders where your bushes end.

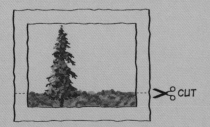
CUT

10. Clip off all four corners of the border surrounding the starry sky artwork, and fold the border back 1 inch. For the remaining two pieces, clip off only the two bottom corners of the borders and fold the bottom and side borders back 1 inch.

11. Insert the starry sky into the box at the end opposite the peephole, with your picture facing the hole.

12. Insert your city scene a few inches in front of the starry sky.

13. Insert your shrubbery scene in front of the city scene.

14. Look through the peephole to test how the scenes line up. If you can easily see them all, tape their folded edges to the sides of the box. If not, move them forward or backward in the box until they are in a good position. If the folded borders show, paint them blue.

15. Cut a piece of wax paper large enough to cover the hole in the shoebox lid. Tape it to the underside of the lid.

16. Place the lid on the box. Look into the peephole, and enter your magical land.

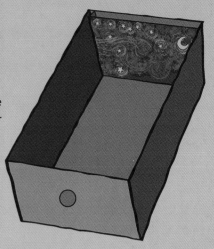

ART AS THERAPY

IT UPSET VAN GOGH that the patients at Saint-Paul-de-Mausole had no daily activities; some institutions encouraged gardening, for example. Eating and playing checkers seemed to be all they could look forward to. Van Gogh was thankful he had his art.

Today, Saint-Paul-de-Mausole is still a psychiatric institution, and art therapy is available to patients who live there. A lovely gallery exhibits their remarkable work. At the top of the gallery's Romanesque stairway, visitors can see the wheat field that van Gogh contemplated and painted during his stay.

With Dr. Peyron's permission, he began to explore the surrounding area, too. In case van Gogh became ill during an excursion, an attendant was assigned to go with him. The charming village of St. Rémy was within walking distance, and at times van Gogh ventured there. Outside of town, the countryside was dotted with olive groves, fields of wheat, and vineyards. Two miles away, rocky cliffs called the Alpilles sprang up. The hilly landscape was different from the flat plains of Arles and had many interesting vistas to paint.

Van Gogh especially admired the cypress trees that grew in the region. To van Gogh, the tall, slender trees were similar to obelisks—the tapering stone pillars built by the Egyptians. He was fascinated by the trees and determined to paint them in a new way. "They have not been done the way I see them," he explained to Theo in a letter. Real cypresses don't have such fiery shapes, but van Gogh transformed the tall, narrow evergreens into flames that flickered up into the sky. To do this, he painted them using swirling, curling brushstrokes.

Very early one morning in June, van Gogh sat looking out his bedroom window. Gazing past the bars, he watched the night sky shimmering above the Alpilles. It was long before sunrise, and the morning star was shining bright. He had been thinking about painting a night sky as he had done in Arles. But, he thought, he could do it better. The result is one of van Gogh's most famous paintings, *The Starry Night*.

In his painting, van Gogh captured the mountain scene he saw out his window, which was complete with stars and cypress trees. Although his stars glow with fanciful swirls of color, he accurately depicted the constellations and planets that shone in the night sky in June 1889. When he added the village nestled at the foot of the mountains, he used his imagination. The church, with its tall steeple, isn't the type you'd see in southern France. Van Gogh was feeling lonely, remembering his childhood in the Netherlands. His little town is a "memory of the North," a Dutch village.

After he finished and the paint was dry, van Gogh sent *Starry Night* to his brother. Theo recognized it as a shared memory from their childhood. When he wrote to van Gogh, he referred to the picture as "the village in the moonlight."

By July, van Gogh had completed an astonishing number of pieces. He painted all day and spent his evenings reading the plays of Shakespeare that Theo had sent him. A letter from Jo brought the exciting news that she was going to have a baby in February. If the baby was a boy, she and Theo planned to name him Vincent.

A RELAPSE

Two months had passed since van Gogh entered the asylum, and he was still feeling fine. Although Dr. Peyron thought he would need to stay there at least a year, van Gogh wondered if he were cured.

Soon after, while working in the fields on a windy day, he was stricken by an attack. He began hallucinating and tried to eat his paints, which were poisonous. Luckily, his attendant restrained him before he could harm himself.

He suffered agonizing hallucinations for the next five weeks. When he recovered, van Gogh felt weak and demoralized. As a result, he wouldn't leave his bedroom for two months. When he finally felt well enough to work, Dr. Peyron refused to give him his paints. He was afraid van Gogh might try eating them again. Van Gogh asked Theo to write to the doctor, explaining how important it was for him to be able to paint. "Working on my paintings is almost a necessity for my recovery," he told Theo, "for these days without anything to do . . . are almost unbearable." Dr. Peyron eventually returned his paints.

At first van Gogh worked only in his studio. For subject matter he once again turned to himself, painting two self-portraits. In one of them, his red hair and beard stand out against pale blues and greens. The background of furious swirls suggests the turmoil from which he had just emerged.

During the next eight months, van Gogh suffered several attacks. Some were short, lasting only a week, while the longest gripped him for two months. During one spell, he tried to drink the kerosene that was used to fill lamps in the asylum. Once again, an attendant

Create a Self-Portrait in Swirling Words

Van Gogh painted over 30 self-portraits in his lifetime. Of them, his portrait made up of swirling lines of blues and greens is probably his best known. Paint a self-portrait using van Gogh's color scheme, and express your thoughts in swirling words.

MATERIALS

Writing paper	Watercolor paints
Pencil	Paintbrush
Mirror	Container of water
Heavy drawing paper	Black China marker

1. Make a list of at least 20 words or phrases that describe your world. Here are some ideas to get you started:
   - List the names of your friends, pets, and family members.
   - What are the things you love and the things you hate?
   - What are your favorite foods, music, and hobbies?
   - If you were granted three wishes, what would they be?

2. On a piece of drawing paper, sketch a portrait of yourself lightly in pencil. Look into a mirror as you draw, and include your head, shoulders, and chest.

3. Notice how van Gogh's background is made up of swirling lines. Using a pencil, lightly draw swirling lines in the background of your picture. You will write words on some of the lines, so allow space between them.

4. Follow van Gogh's blue, green, and lavender color scheme to paint your portrait in watercolors. Do not color the background.

5. Using a China marker, fill the background with words from your list. Write them along the swirling pencil lines. If your words do not fill a line, add dots between thoughts. For example: I love to play baseball . . . . . Let's Dance! . . . . Hot Fudge Sundaes.

6. Use watercolors to paint swirls of blue and green on top of your words.

VINCENT VAN GOGH

Self-Portrait, 1889

72

was able to stop him. Between these crises, van Gogh was perfectly lucid. He painted wonderful pictures, visited Arles, and wrote many letters to family members and friends.

GOOD NEWS

In February, van Gogh received news that he was an uncle. Jo had given birth to a boy, and, as promised, she and Theo named him Vincent. To celebrate, van Gogh painted a stunning picture of almond branches against a bright blue sky. It was the first tree to blossom in spring, symbolizing birth to him. The flowering branches seem to sway overhead, as if the viewer is looking up through its branches into the sky. Van Gogh wanted Theo to hang the picture next to Vincent's cradle, so he could look up at the branches.

Van Gogh received other news, too. A young critic named Albert Aurier had seen his paintings at Theo's apartment and Tanguy's shop and had written a glowing article about them. Published in a magazine called *Le Mercure de France*, the review praised the work for its "dazzling symphonies of color and lines" and called van Gogh "a terrible maddened genius." At last, his talent was acknowledged.

But instead of being happy about finally being recognized, van Gogh was upset. "Please ask Mr. Aurier not to write any more articles on my painting," he wrote to Theo. "It pains me more than he knows." It wasn't being called mad that upset him. It was that Aurier

had been too flattering to him. Van Gogh thought that other artists, like Gauguin, deserved the praise more than he did.

While in St. Rémy, several representatives asked van Gogh to send paintings to art exhibitions. In January, an exhibition by a group called Les XX opened in Brussels and included six of his paintings. Shortly after, Theo wrote to tell him that one of his paintings had sold! *The Red Vineyard*, which he had painted in Arles, had sold for the decent price of 400 francs. The woman who purchased it, Anna Boch, was an artist herself. Her brother, Eugène Boch, had met van Gogh during the summer while visiting Arles and had posed for a portrait.

The show was not without some dramatic moments. Toulouse-Lautrec overheard a Belgian artist call van Gogh's paintings the work of an ignoramus. Lautrec flamboyantly challenged the Belgian to a duel. It was called off when Lautrec's friends put a stop to it.

IN SEARCH OF A NEW HOME

Van Gogh realized that Dr. Peyron could not cure his ailments. He also began to think that the other patients had a bad effect on him. Being cooped up with them was "a dangerous thing, in which you risk losing the little good sense that you may still have kept." As spring approached, he became more and more determined to leave. The problem was, where would he go?

He knew he could not live alone. He also couldn't live with Theo, who now had a wife and baby and

VINCENT VAN GOGH

Branch of an Almond Tree in Blossom, 1890

was often ill himself. Gauguin was living in Brittany. When van Gogh wrote to suggest he join him there, Gauguin politely refused. Later, to his friends, Gauguin exclaimed, "Not that man! He tried to kill me!" Camille Pissarro, the fatherly Impressionist, wanted to help, but his wife refused. She wouldn't allow van Gogh to stay with them, fearing for her children's safety.

Pissarro thought of another plan. His friend Paul Gachet was a physician who had experience with patients suffering from nervous disorders. He was an art enthusiast as well. Dr. Gachet lived in Auvers-sur-Oise, a village near Paris. He'd be willing to keep an eye on van Gogh if he moved there.

Van Gogh was enthusiastic about the idea. Auvers had been the home of one of his favorite painters, Charles-François Daubigny. He knew the area would be full of subjects to paint—both Pissarro and Cézanne had worked there, too. Most of all, van Gogh was relieved that the doctor would be nearby. If he had another attack, Gachet would be there to prevent the police from locking him up.

RETURNING NORTH

A year after he entered the asylum, 37-year-old van Gogh left Provence for Auvers. Along the way, he visited Theo. When he arrived at the train station in Paris, Theo was waiting for him. They took an open carriage to his fourth-floor apartment, where Jo was waiting for them with baby Vincent.

Jo was thrilled to finally meet Theo's older brother and surprised to see how healthy he looked. She couldn't help but compare the two brothers, noting that Vincent looked healthier than her husband. Theo took van Gogh in to see the baby, who was asleep in his cradle. They stood there without saying anything, both with tears in their eyes.

The apartment overflowed with van Gogh's paintings. They hung on walls, were spread on the floor, and stacked under the bed. Later, the brothers walked over to Tanguy's shop. Over the years, van Gogh had traded paintings with other artists, such as Bernard and Gauguin. These, along with some of his own, were stored in Tanguy's attic. It had been over two years since the brothers were able to stand together to talk about them.

After three days in Paris, van Gogh felt agitated by the noise and bustle of the big city. He decided to go on to Auvers, hoping Theo and Jo would visit him soon. His stay with Jo and Theo had been pleasant, but van Gogh was not entirely pleased with Theo.

Once in Auvers, he wrote to Theo, listing his problems. He was upset about how Theo was taking care of his paintings. Stacking canvases, some with paint as thick as half an inch on them, was causing the paint to crack. He didn't think Tanguy's attic was a suitable storage space either, calling it a "bedbug infested hole." In addition, he wasn't clear whether Theo intended to support him in the same manner he had in the past. Nothing had been settled about his monthly allowance.

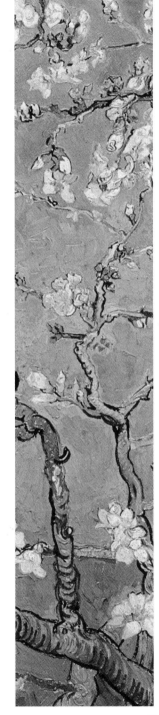

A CLOSER LOOK
DR. GACHET

VINCENT VAN GOGH

Portrait of Dr. Gachet, 1890

THE IDEA OF PAINTING Gachet's portrait occurred to van Gogh the day they met. Over the next two weeks, he planned how he would portray him.

The painting is a study in complementary colors. Gachet's orange hair is contrasted by his blue jacket and a lighter blue background. He leans on a red table, which complements the green leaves of the flower he holds. The flower is a foxglove, used to make a medicine called digitalis. Van Gogh included it in the picture as a symbol of Gachet's medical profession.

The portrait expresses the tenderness van Gogh felt toward him. It also tells us something about who Gachet was. The most striking feature of the portrait is the doctor's sad expression. Van Gogh didn't want to portray Gachet in a traditional way—one that would glorify him. He wanted people who looked at the painting years later to understand something about Gachet's personality. In his face, van Gogh saw "the heartbroken expression of our time."

As he often did, van Gogh painted two versions of the portrait. He gave the second version (shown here) as a gift to Gachet in thanks for his friendship. The first version included two books on the table. In 1990, that version sold for $82.5 million. At the time, it was the highest price ever paid for a painting.

In reply, Theo reassured him that he would send 150 francs a month—a comfortable amount. Tanguy helped by offering to carefully pack up the paintings and send them to van Gogh.

DR. GACHET

Van Gogh arrived in Auvers and rented a room on the third floor of an inn owned by the Ravoux family. He was eager to meet Gachet, who sounded perfect as both a physician and friend. As a student, Gachet had worked in two asylums. He had even written a thesis on melancholia, which is called depression today. Although his practice wasn't limited to mental illness, Gachet had experience with patients who suffered from nervous disorders.

In spite of the doctor's credentials, van Gogh was disappointed when he met him. He found the 61-year-old doctor aging and out of touch. In fact, Gachet seemed to be suffering from nervous troubles himself. It made van Gogh wonder which of them was more ill. Gachet was sympathetic toward van Gogh but more interested in him as an artist than a patient.

Gachet was an art lover. He was especially enthusiastic about new styles and owned works by Monet, Pissarro, Cézanne, and others. An amateur artist himself, he not only painted but also made etchings printed on his own press. After praising van Gogh's canvases, the doctor dismissed the seriousness of his illness. He advised van Gogh to work as hard as he could and forget about his problems.

VINCENT VAN GOGH

Stairway at Auvers, 1890 (detail)

Despite his disappointment in Gachet as a physician, van Gogh liked him as a friend. Over the next two months, he visited the doctor often at his home. Gachet was a widower and lived in a big, gloomy house with his 20-year-old daughter, Marguerite, and 16-year-old son, Paul.

One of the first paintings van Gogh made in Auvers was Gachet's portrait. It's not obvious, but the doctor posed for van Gogh in his garden. Van Gogh enjoyed painting in Gachet's rambling garden, which held a menagerie of animals: eight cats, eight dogs, a peacock, and numerous chickens, rabbits, and ducks. He couldn't paint at his room in the inn because it was so small, but he had an open invitation to set up his easel at Gachet's.

Van Gogh saw why Auvers attracted other artists. It was full of beautiful and interesting sights. The village was situated in a narrow valley along a river. Cliffs rose up to a plateau where wheat fields overlooked the town. The streets curved every which way, and steps connected one level of town to the next. Outside the village, bright yellow fields of wheat swayed in the breeze. Above the fields was the bright blue sky.

The first Sunday in June, Theo and Jo came to visit. Van Gogh met them at the train station, bringing along a bird's nest as a gift for baby Vincent. Gachet invited them for lunch in his garden, where van Gogh insisted on carrying his nephew around the property, happily introducing him to all the animals. It was a wonderful day for van Gogh.

PROBLEMS IN PARIS

Later that month, Theo sent a letter that announced some disturbing news. The baby had fallen seriously ill, probably the result of drinking contaminated milk. Vincent was expected to live, but his days and nights of endless crying had left Theo and Jo exhausted. Stressed to the breaking point, Theo went on to reveal other concerns that he normally would have hidden from his brother.

He complained bitterly about his employers at the gallery. For quite some time, they had refused to give him a much-needed and deserved raise. Although he was a valuable employee who had been with them for years, they treated him terribly. Theo was fed up and ready to resign. It was upsetting news for van Gogh. Knowing Theo was stressed financially, he worried that he was part of the problem.

When the baby's health improved, van Gogh went to Paris to visit the family. When he saw Theo, it was obvious that his lack of money and the stress of his job were affecting his health. Vincent realized it had been a mistake to come to Paris. Worn out from caring for a sick baby, Theo and Jo's nerves were on end. They fought constantly, arguing about where to hang a painting, moving to a bigger apartment, and whether Theo should quit his job. Jo was against it.

In his brother's honor, Theo had invited a few friends for lunch that day. Among the guests were art critic Albert Aurier and painter Toulouse-Lautrec. Van Gogh was happy to see his friends, but the lunch didn't go well. Tension was so high that not even Lautrec's good humor could ease it. Van Gogh had planned to stay in Paris for three days, but he left that same day.

When he returned home, he wrote a letter to Theo and Jo. He discussed the visit and admitted his anxiety about the future. They both replied, trying to reassure him that everything would be fine. But their words didn't

WHEATFIELD WITH CROWS

DURING THE 70 DAYS van Gogh lived in Auvers, he produced more than 70 paintings. One of his last, *Wheatfield with Crows*, reflects his turbulent state of mind. In it, black crows hover over a landscape in turmoil. Broken, staccato jabs have replaced the spiraling brush strokes he used in St. Rémy. Three red paths crisscross, slashing through the wheat. Above, the sky is dark and stormy.

VINCENT VAN GOGH
Wheatfield with Crows, 1890

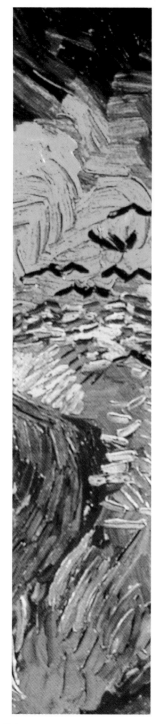

make him feel any better. Van Gogh wrote back, saying he felt he was a burden on them, "a thing to be dreaded."

It's not certain that van Gogh's concerns caused the events that followed, but they clearly played a role. He continued painting, but slowly his nerves began to fray.

On Sunday, July 27, van Gogh set off toward the wheat fields he had painted so often. This time, he carried a gun. He needed it, he told the person he borrowed it from, to scare crows. Walking into a field, he turned it on himself. The bullet entered his chest but did not kill him.

Doubled up with pain, he managed to walk back to the inn. Ravoux, the owner, was standing outside talking with Anton Hirschig, another artist who was staying at the inn. They watched as van Gogh climbed the stairs to his attic room. Disturbed by van Gogh's late return and strange behavior, Ravoux went to his room. He found van Gogh in bed, his face to the wall. "I shot myself," he said softly. "I only hope I haven't botched it."

The local physician was summoned, and van Gogh also asked for Gachet. The doctors agreed that it would be impossible to remove the bullet.

Gachet wanted to inform Theo, but van Gogh refused to give them his home address. As a result, he didn't get word until the next day, when Hirschig brought a letter to him at the gallery.

When Theo arrived at the inn later that morning, he found his brother lying in bed, smoking his pipe. Because he was conscious, Theo thought van Gogh would be OK. That day and into the next, he stayed by

his side. At 1:30 A.M. on July 29, 1890, van Gogh died. He was 37 years old.

A LAST FAREWELL

Van Gogh's funeral took place the next day. Because he had committed suicide, the local Catholic church refused to hold it there. Instead it was held at the inn. Eight friends gathered to say good-bye, including Émile Bernard, Andries Bonger, and Père Tanguy. Bernard later described the scene: "The coffin was already closed. I arrived too late to see him again. . . . On the walls of the room where the body lay all his last canvases were nailed, forming something like a halo. . . . On the coffin a simple white drapery, then masses of flowers, sunflowers which he loved so much, yellow dahlias, yellow flowers everywhere." His easel, folding stool, and brushes were set alongside.

At three o'clock a horse-drawn hearse came for van Gogh. His friends walked up the hill to the cemetery. Gachet tried to say a few words at the grave but wept so much he could only stammer a brief farewell. Theo was broken with grief. After his brother's death, Theo found a letter written to him in van Gogh's pocket. It was possibly a draft of one he received earlier, describing how important Theo had been for van Gogh's painting.

Shattered by his brother's death, Theo never recovered. After the funeral, he began planning a memorial exhibition of van Gogh's work. He rented a larger apartment in his building and asked Bernard to help him arrange the display. Bernard helped choose the paintings and painted a shepherd scene on the living room windows, making them look like medieval stained glass. Theo's apartment became a museum dedicated to his brother's memory. He was determined to gain recognition of van Gogh's exceptional genius.

Sadly, he was unable to achieve his goal. Theo's health, which had been fragile for years, quickly deteriorated. Like his brother, he was suffering from mental as well as physical disorders. In November, he was admitted to a psychiatric clinic in Holland. Six months after his brother's suicide, Theo died at age 33. Today, he rests alongside van Gogh in the little cemetery in Auvers.

WHAT VAN GOGH LEFT BEHIND

Van Gogh's 10 years of artistic effort produced nearly 900 paintings and 1,100 drawings. The fact that so many are considered masterpieces today is a tribute to his extraordinary drive, focus, and talent.

As time went on, van Gogh's fame grew. His unique approach to painting had a strong influence on the next generation of artists. Henri Matisse and his group, the Fauves, took van Gogh's ideas about color a step further.

Another group, the Expressionists, was inspired by the emotion found in van Gogh's work. These artists thought it more important to paint their feelings about a subject rather than how it actually looked. Paintings like *The Starry Night* gave them ideas about how to do this.

Today several of van Gogh's paintings rank among the most expensive paintings in the world. In 1987, his

ART DETECTIVE
How to Spot a van Gogh

Here are some characteristics that help distinguish van Gogh's work:

* **Swirls and curls!** Skies made of swirling colors, trees made of curling strokes

* **Complementary colors!** Often orange next to blue

* **Sunflowers!** Vases full of huge yellow blooms, heads drooping this way and that

* **Portraits!** Everyday people in humble poses

* **Self-portraits!** Orange hair, beard, and mustache, often set against a blue background

* **Night skies!** Glowing yellow and orange stars in blue-violet skies

Irises sold at a Sotheby's auction for $53.9 million. This was topped in 1990, when his *Portrait of Dr. Gachet* sold at a Christie's auction for a record-breaking $82.5 million.

Van Gogh has touched the lives of many people. His art captured the minds and hearts of millions of art lovers. He's also made art lovers of newcomers to the world of art.

JOHANNA VAN GOGH

AFTER THEO'S DEATH, some family members thought Jo should throw van Gogh's paintings out and get on with her life. But she refused to abandon the work that had meant so much to her husband and his brother. She continued their fight and succeeded.

On her first evening alone in the apartment, Jo took out the letters that Theo had collected over the years. Night after night, she read them to ease her grief. Over time, she cataloged more than 680 letters and arranged for them to be published.

Unable to bear the sad memories the Paris apartment held, Jo moved back to Holland. She opened a boardinghouse and decorated it with dozens of van Gogh's paintings. Jo then focused on organizing exhibitions. One of the first opened in 1892 with the help of Bernard. A larger exhibition in 1901 won the attention of artists like Henri Matisse, along with the Parisian public. The value of the works gradually began to increase. To meet her living expenses and to promote van Gogh's reputation, Jo sold some of the pieces. Still, when she died in 1925, the collection had over 700 works.

Next, van Gogh's nephew Vincent took charge. In 1930, he moved the collection to the Stedelijk Museum in Amsterdam. When World War II broke out in 1939, the paintings were hidden in bunkers on the Dutch coast for safekeeping. (Van Gogh's Yellow House in Arles was not so lucky. In 1944 the little building was hit in a bombing raid, his bedroom reduced to rubble.)

In 1973, a museum built specially for the collection opened in Amsterdam. Along with his paintings, drawings, and letters, the Van Gogh Museum houses his Japanese prints, personal items such as family photographs, and paintings done by his artist friends.

PAUL GAUGUIN

Portrait of the Artist with the Idol, ca. 1893

6 Paul Gauguin

PAUL GAUGUIN WAS IN Brittany when he learned of van Gogh's death. He immediately wrote a cordial note to Theo.

Two years before, while van Gogh was preparing for his visit, Gauguin had been painting on Brittany's rocky coast. He had just finished what was surely a masterpiece and had big plans for it.

The painting, which he called *The Vision After the Sermon*, had a religious theme. What better place to hang the painting, he thought, than a church? The perfect one, built in medieval times, was two miles away. So in late September 1888, villagers in Pont-Aven may have noticed three paint-stained artists toting a large parcel up the hillside toward the ancient church.

The fact that the church's priest hadn't seen the painting and didn't know it was coming didn't faze Gauguin. He was sure he would take one look and be sold on it. Inside the church Gauguin's two accomplices, Émile Bernard and Charles Laval, positioned the canvas just as Gauguin wished and then went to fetch the priest. He was not impressed. Defeated, the three artists lugged the painting home.

Luckily Gauguin had a back-up plan. He sent the painting off to Theo van Gogh. Theo would find someone who recognized his genius! With that, he packed his bags and boarded a train for Arles. Little did Gauguin know how *this* venture would turn out.

AN EXCITING BEGINNING

Eugène-Henri Paul Gauguin was born on June 7, 1848, in the heart of Paris. Outside on the streets, a battle was raging. Citizens were rebelling because there were no jobs and the people were starving. Later that year, Louis-Napoléon Bonaparte was elected president. (Unable to run for a second term, he later declared himself Emperor Napoléon III.)

Louis-Napoléon's election mattered a great deal to the Gauguin family. Gauguin's father, a political writer, wrote articles criticizing the new president. This was a risky stand to take, one that could lead to being thrown in prison. So Mr. Gauguin decided a year later to move his family to South America. Paul was only one year old when his family took a ship to Lima, Peru.

GROWING UP IN PERU

Paul's mother had a wealthy relative named Pio, who lived in Lima. His father hoped Uncle Pio would help him start his own newspaper there. Sadly, Paul's father died during the long journey across the ocean. Instead of arriving in Lima excited about the future, Paul's mother arrived a poor widow, alone in a strange land with two small children. Luckily Uncle Pio was thrilled to add the three newcomers to his large family. His house was one of the biggest in Lima, and there was room for everyone.

Peru was very different from France—children had monkeys for pets! The family didn't worry about thunderstorms because it hardly ever rained, but they grew used to waking up in shaking beds because of the frequent earthquakes. Young Paul loved growing up there. He was able to meet people he would never have known

in France; Chinese, Native Americans, and Africans were a part of his daily life. France seemed very far away to this little boy who only spoke Spanish.

Paul lived in South America for five exciting years. When he was seven years old, his mother thought it was time for him to go to school in his native country, so they boarded a ship for the long journey back to France.

Paul enrolled at a boarding school in Orleans, a city south of Paris. He didn't like his new home or school and couldn't even speak French. Because the other students didn't share the interesting experiences of his childhood, Paul decided they were ordinary. They were only the children of common shopkeepers, he thought. Paul wasn't a very good student, not because he wasn't smart but because he was so arrogant. He was so sure that he was better than all the other students that he never even bothered to study. His high opinion of himself didn't win him many friends.

SAILING AWAY

Paul had one dream—he wanted to be a sailor. When he was 17 years old, he quit school and joined the merchant marines. Later, he joined the French navy. For six years Gauguin sailed the oceans, visiting interesting ports all over the world. At age 23 he decided to settle down. But what would he do for a job?

The answer came from a friend of his mother's named Gustave Arosa. Arosa was a wealthy Parisian businessman, a talented photographer, and a patron of the arts. He owned a large collection of paintings by some of the finest artists of the time. Arosa found Gauguin a job in Paris working for a stockbroker.

Even though Gauguin had no experience or training, he soon became very good at his job. It wasn't long before he was making a very good living for himself. He became a rich and respected broker.

Life outside of his job was quiet. Gauguin's favorite pastime was reading. One day a friend from work, Émile Schuffenecker (Schuff, for short), sparked his interest in another hobby—painting.

A SUNDAY PAINTER

Gauguin immersed himself in his new hobby. Sometimes he and Schuff went on art outings. They'd go to the Louvre or visit art galleries. Often on Sundays they took their paint boxes and easels to the countryside outside Paris. Once in a while they even took an art lesson. It was all great fun for Gauguin. With his puffed-up ego, he liked hearing others admire his work.

One day he met a girl named Mette Gad who was on vacation in Paris. Gauguin was immediately attracted to the tall, 22-year-old Danish girl. As for Gad, the more she learned about Gauguin, the more she liked him. He had such an interesting past, she thought. And now he was a wealthy stockbroker! A year later they married. But in all that time, Gauguin didn't mention to Gad his interest in painting. Strangely, he waited until after they were married to tell her.

PAUL GAUGUIN
Women Bathing, 1885

At first, Mette didn't mind her husband's painting. She didn't realize that it was more than just a hobby. As time went on, it became all Gauguin thought about. Three years after their marriage, he entered one of his landscape paintings at the annual Salon. Not only was it accepted, but the critics liked it!

Meanwhile, Mette watched with growing concern as Gauguin's hobby turned into a fixation. She tried to remind him of his duties as a husband and a father—they now had a son. But her complaints had no effect; he just

THE SALON

IN 1876, WHEN GAUGUIN exhibited his painting at the Salon, it was the grandest art exhibition in the Western world. The jury chose as many as 4,000 works to be shown. The Salon lasted two months and was visited by art dealers, critics, and wealthy collectors from all over the world.

spent more time painting. Gauguin tried to communicate his love for painting to his wife without success.

One day, while visiting Arosa, Gauguin was introduced to another guest—the Impressionist artist Camille Pissarro. Like Arosa, Gauguin had started to collect art, purchasing paintings by Cézanne, Monet, Renoir, and Pissarro. When Pissarro heard that Gauguin was interested in painting, he invited Gauguin to paint with him. Soon Pissarro became Gauguin's art teacher, and his first lesson was to use pure, bright colors.

They also went to a Paris café where the modern painters and writers met to discuss their ideas. Not all of them welcomed the newcomer. Monet didn't care for

Gauguin and made little secret of it. He said he didn't approve of amateurs mixing with professionals. Edgar Degas, on the other hand, enjoyed Gauguin's company, perhaps because they were both a bit arrogant. Cézanne, who was always suspicious, absolutely hated Gauguin. "This fool of a Sunday painter is trying to filch hard-won secrets," he protested.

Nonetheless, Pissarro and Degas invited this Sunday painter to exhibit with the Impressionists. His debut exhibiting with the Impressionists was at the Fourth Impressionist Exhibition in 1879, where he submitted a sculpture. The next year he exhibited six paintings. Over the next few years, he continued to paint, sculpted, and took up ceramics. "One day," he dreamed, "I'll become a full-time artist."

LIFE AS AN ARTIST

An unexpected event made Gauguin's decision about being an artist much easier. In 1882 the Union General bank crashed, causing a collapse in the stock market. Gauguin's income also decreased. Several months later he decided to quit. "From now on I paint every day," he declared when he got home. His wife was shocked. After all, her 35-year-old husband had a family to support—they now had five children. But Gauguin couldn't imagine failing at anything he tried, and he was sure he would be an immediate success. Unfortunately, he was mistaken. Life as an artist was a tremendous struggle, and within a year their savings were used up. Angry,

Mette moved back to Denmark with their children. She took a job there teaching French.

Penniless, Gauguin became dependent on Schuff and a few others who occasionally offered him hospitality and loans. Despite the setbacks and humiliations, Gauguin never wavered from his devotion to art. He was convinced he would eventually receive the recognition he deserved. He dreamed of traveling to a primitive place with a warm, sunny climate. There he could live off the land and paint wonderful pictures. Eventually he was able to raise enough money to move to his tropical paradise—the island of Martinique. This Caribbean island, with its brilliant colors and friendly natives, delighted him. Another artist, Charles Laval, joined him on his adventure. They lived in a hut overlooking the sea, a setting Gauguin described as paradise. There was one serious problem, however. The damp, tropical climate proved devastating for Gauguin's health. He caught malaria, a debilitating disease that is transmitted by the bite of a mosquito. Gauguin suffered terrible attacks of chills and fevers, along with abdominal pain and diarrhea from an intestinal disease called dysentery. He had to return to France for medical treatment. Laval, who was even sicker, was not strong enough to travel and returned several months later.

Even though Gauguin's time in Martinique was short, it marked a turning point in his art. He completed several luminous paintings in a style that would soon be recognized as uniquely his own.

THE VAN GOGH BROTHERS

Soon after Gauguin returned from Martinique, he met Theo and Vincent van Gogh. Gauguin's first impression was how different the two brothers were. They looked alike—could almost be twins—but there the similarity ended. One was a smartly dressed businessman, calmly examining the paintings Gauguin set out for them. The other was jerky, scruffy, and madly excited about the works.

The meeting was a great success; Theo bought three of the paintings. As for Vincent, he was dazzled by Gauguin's stories about his tropical adventure. It was most likely then that he hatched his plan to get Gauguin to join him in Arles. After all, it too was warm, sunny, and full of interesting sights to paint.

The same month van Gogh moved to southern France, Gauguin headed for its western coast, to a region called Brittany. It was his second visit to the beautiful area where artists from all over the world came to paint. Sunny memories of his days in Martinique began to appear in his paintings. Gauguin loved bright colors. He used these colors even if he wasn't painting a brightly lit scene.

That summer, van Gogh's friend Émile Bernard also visited Brittany. Bernard was only 20, and he regarded 40-year-old Gauguin as a masterful artist. They became close friends, painting and discussing art together. Bernard liked to visit medieval churches to study their beautiful stained glass windows. His paintings resembled the windows, with brilliant flat colors outlined in

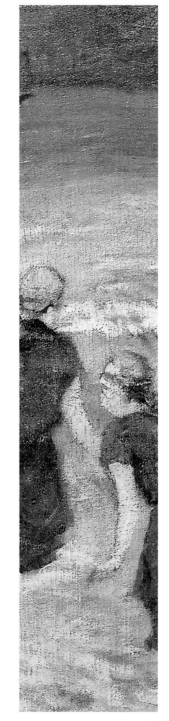

THE VISION AFTER THE SERMON

In *The Vision After the Sermon*, Gauguin painted a group of Breton women praying. The big white bonnets were part of their traditional costumes, but everything else in the painting comes from Gauguin's imagination. The women are praying but there is no one delivering a sermon. Instead, Gauguin painted what the listeners might imagine after hearing a sermon on the Bible story about Jacob wrestling with an angel. Gauguin colored the grass bright red and added a tiny, prancing cow.

This is the painting Gauguin thought the local priest would be thrilled to purchase for his church. The priest, however, flatly refused. When it was exhibited in 1889, some people thought Gauguin painted it just to be shocking. Others thought it was a truly original work of art.

PAUL GAUGUIN

The Vision After the Sermon, 1888

Draw a Dreamscape

Create a picture using Gauguin's method by combining what is real (you!) with what you imagine.

MATERIALS

Your favorite book

Pencil

Drawing paper

Eraser

Coloring supplies

1. Reread a scene from your favorite book, then close your eyes and imagine what it looks like. Picture details like what the characters are wearing and the setting.

2. Using a pencil, draw a picture of yourself reading the book. There are many settings in which you could place yourself. For example: in an armchair next to a big window, leaning against a tree on a hillside, or in bed at night with a flashlight. Draw the book so that its cover shows, including its title.

3. Add the scene from your story somewhere in the picture. For instance: as if it is happening outside the window you are sitting next to, on the distant horizon of the hillside you are visiting, or surrounding your bed.

4. Add color to your dreamscape picture.

Try Another Style: Write your own short story. Draw a scene from the story, and include yourself writing the story instead of reading a book.

Activity

Start the (You) School

Start an art group with your friends, and give it a name that's all your own: the (You) School. Get together to make craft projects, put on puppet plays, and party! School was never so much fun.

MATERIALS

A group of friends

A meeting place

Art supplies

1. Ask a few of your artsy friends to join you in a weekly or monthly get-together to celebrate your creative sides.

2. Think of a name for your group. It should be something that describes who you are as a group. It could be the type of art you like to make: the Glitter Glue School, for example.

3. Each time you get together, try something new. Decide what you'll do and bring the supplies you'll need. One time you can paint, the next time make a peep box, or bring your beading supplies and make bracelets. Take turns sharing your knowledge. If someone knows a certain craft, like origami, he or she can teach everyone else.

4. Don't limit yourself to art projects. Make a Shadow Puppet Theater and put on a play. Or borrow a video camera and make a movie. Explore your creative side—and have fun.

5. Hold an exhibition! Display your work, and put on a puppet play or show your movie during the event.

black. Soon both artists were using this technique. They were also influenced by other art forms such as folk art, tapestries, and Japanese prints. They experimented with perspective using techniques from these works.

Gauguin thought a painting should do more than just show a scene. It should also express how the artist felt about the scene. "Don't copy nature too literally," he wrote in a letter to Schuff. "Draw art from nature as you dream in nature's presence." Along with the unnatural colors he chose, Gauguin added imaginary elements to his paintings. His painting *The Vision After the Sermon* is a perfect example.

THE PONT-AVEN SCHOOL

The village where Gauguin stayed during this time is called Pont-Aven. Other painters staying in the village admired Gauguin's work so much that they began to paint in a similar style. They became known as the Pont-Aven School, and Gauguin was their leader.

The postman must have been busy that summer in Pont-Aven. Even though van Gogh was painting on his own, a two-day train ride away, he diligently kept in touch with his friends. They wrote to each other so often and in such detail about their art, he was practically a member of their group. Eager to see what they were up to, van Gogh suggested that Gauguin, Bernard, and Laval paint each other's portraits to exchange. They decided instead to all paint themselves. Van Gogh and Gauguin exchanged self-portraits. When it arrived, van

Gogh brought the portrait to his favorite café. Showing it to the owner, he proudly announced that Gauguin would be coming to Arles any day!

A VISIT TO THE SOUTH OF FRANCE

Van Gogh admired Gauguin immensely and was thrilled when he finally agreed to come to Arles. Had van Gogh been less enthusiastic and more cautious, he would have known it was a bad idea. Earlier that year, an art critic name Félix Fénéon had written an article about Gauguin. He observed that Gauguin had a disagreeable personality. It was the first time Gauguin's aggressive, arrogant manner had been mentioned in print. Living under one roof with the unstable van Gogh was bound to come to a bad end. Still, during the two months that they painted together, they influenced each other's work.

Gauguin was back in Brittany when he learned of van Gogh's death 19 months later. He sent a letter of condolence to Theo but otherwise didn't appear especially affected by the news. Later, when Bernard tried to organize a memorial exhibition of van Gogh's work, Gauguin disapproved. He thought it would harm them all to promote the idea that important art could be produced by a madman.

OFF TO TAHITI

In 1891, Gauguin returned to the tropics. This time he went to Tahiti. He would live in the islands, off and on, for the rest of his life. He always hoped he'd be wealthy

PAUL GAUGUIN

Piti Teina (Two Sisters), 1892

93

How to Spot a Gauguin

Here are some characteristics that help distinguish Gauguin's work:

※ **Bright, flat colors!** Often outlined in black

※ **Unnatural colors!** They turn up in unexpected places

※ **Big white bonnets!** Women in Brittany wore this type of hat

※ **Writing on pictures!** Often the picture's title is written somewhere on the painting

※ **Tropical scenes!** His favorite subjects include palm trees, native girls, and island motifs

Back in Europe, most people failed to understand his art and, as a result, didn't like his paintings. The reaction of the critics was a bit more encouraging. But some of them weren't ready for his use of unnatural colors either. They made fun of his mustard-colored seas and vivid blue tree trunks.

Gauguin spent the last years of his life in poverty and pain. He broke his leg in a brawl during his last visit to France and became dependent on morphine and alcohol to escape the excruciating pain. After suffering a series of heart attacks, Gauguin died at the age of 54. He was buried in a cemetery on Hiva Oa, the last island he called home. It took three months for the word of Gauguin's death to reach Paris.

GAUGUIN'S LEGEND LIVES ON

Five months after Gauguin's death, Vollard held an exhibition of his work. The public learned that Gauguin was far more than a colorful, exotic legend. His paintings and drawings revealed him to be an immensely powerful and strikingly original artist. Since that time, Gauguin's fame has grown even more. His bold use of color and form has influenced many of the artists who followed him. Today, Gauguin is considered one of the most important contributors to modern art. He is remembered as an innovator, a courageous painter who dared to experiment.

again and his family would join him in his tropical paradise. It was a dream that would never come true. Before leaving Paris he hired an art dealer, Ambroise Vollard, to sell his work. Gauguin occasionally sent Mette some money when he sold a painting, but that didn't happen very often.

PAUL GAUGUIN

Nave, Nave, Moe (Delightful Drowsiness), 1894

95

HENRI DE TOULOUSE-LAUTREC

The Seated Clowness, 1896

7 Henri de Toulouse-Lautrec

HENRI DE TOULOUSE-LAUTREC was one artist who was happy to stay in Paris. To him, sketching at a local café was much more interesting than painting sunflowers in Arles or a tropical landscape in Tahiti. Sitting at his favorite table at the Moulin Rouge, he captured the rollicking nightlife of Paris. Over his short lifetime he did travel a bit, but he always returned to the city he loved. His posters and paintings have become the symbol of Paris in the 1890s.

A NOBLE BEGINNING

Henri-Marie-Raymond de Toulouse-Lautrec was born November 24, 1864, in Albi, France. His parents, Count Alphonse and Countess Adèle, came from a long line of French nobility. The Toulouse-Lautrecs were a wealthy and powerful family who had ruled over the region in southern France called Languedoc for hundreds of years. Like most children, Henri grew up hearing stories about knights in shining armor. But these weren't fairy tales—they were stories about his ancestors.

Young Henri spent most of his childhood at his family's many chateaus. He had plenty of cousins for playmates and lots of places to play. Most of all, he liked visiting the estate's stables. He loved horses and looked forward to the day he would be old enough to ride.

His love for horses came from his father, who was passionate about riding. The count liked many kinds of animals and kept some exotic pets. He was especially fond of birds of prey, like owls and hawks. On nice days, he took them for rides in his carriage so they could "get some fresh air."

The count was quite a character. He liked to dress up in outrageous costumes (another trait his son would inherit). Once he horrified his parents by coming to

dinner dressed as a Scottish bagpiper, but wearing a tutu instead of a kilt.

Henri's mother was the complete opposite of her husband. Shy and retiring, the countess enjoyed the quiet company of a good book. After her son's birth, she centered her life around him. While the count tended to ignore his son, she lavished attention on him. Throughout his life, Henri and his mother were very close.

When Henri was three years old, his brother was born. One of the first signs of his artistic talent appeared during his brother's baptism. After the ceremony, as his parents signed the parish register, little Henri wanted to sign, too. When the priest pointed out that he didn't know how to write, Henri replied, "Well then, I'll draw an ox."

Henri was a smart little boy; he could read and write by the time he was four and would certainly have thrived in school. But when his frail baby brother became ill and died, the countess became even more protective of her remaining child and insisted he be tutored at home. When the family moved to Paris four years later, he was thrilled to finally attend class with other children.

TRAGIC ACCIDENTS

When he was 13, Henri slipped on a hardwood floor and broke his left leg. It's not uncommon for children to break an arm or a leg, and it usually doesn't cause undue alarm. But Henri's fracture wouldn't heal, and fifteen months later, he fell and broke his other leg. In spite of operations, exercises, and agonizing therapy, his bones wouldn't mend. Henri suffered from a genetic disorder that was unknown at the time; it prevented his bones from healing properly.

It's thought the disorder was due to the fact that his parents were first cousins. Today it's known that children whose parents are closely related can have serious medical problems. As Henri grew older, the upper part of his body developed normally to adult size. But his legs remained the size of a 14-year-old boy's. He stood 4 feet 11 inches when fully grown and needed a cane to support his short, weak legs.

Henri didn't let his handicap stop him from enjoying life. He couldn't run around and play games with his cousins any longer, but he had many other interests. Instead of becoming an accomplished horseman, as was the family tradition, Henri spent his days sketching. He still loved horses and delighted in drawing them. He took lessons from René Princeteau, an artist who specialized in painting horses and dogs.

THE ART STUDENT

When he was 17, Henri decided to become a professional artist. If he had been a healthy heir to the Lautrec fortune, his father would probably have had other plans for him. But after the accidents, the count lost interest in him completely. He pitied his son for his handicap but was indifferent about his future. He agreed to give Henri a generous allowance and dismissed him from his mind. Henri's mother, however, encouraged his love of

DEGAS'S INFLUENCE

BORN IN 1834, Edgar Degas was 30 years older than Toulouse-Lautrec. By the time they were neighbors, Degas was a celebrated artist, one of the Impressionists.

Unlike his fellow Impressionists, though, Degas preferred painting indoor scenes. Nothing escaped his critical eye, from the most dazzling ballerina to the dreariest laundry woman. Degas captured all these scenes of modern-day Paris in his sketchbooks and created finished pictures later in his studio. Like Toulouse-Lautrec, he was fascinated by scenes of café concerts and cabarets.

Degas had definite ideas about what to include in a picture and how to arrange a scene. When he painted *Café-Concert at Les Ambassadeurs*, he included the audience and orchestra, as well as the stage performers. Degas also thought a painting was more interesting if figures were cut off, or cropped, at the edge of the picture—like the man wearing a top hat on the bottom left of this painting.

Toulouse-Lautrec admired Degas's style immensely. Many of the subjects they painted were similar, and he used Degas's cropping technique, too.

EDGAR DEGAS

Café-Concert at Les Ambassadeurs, c. 1876–77

SUZANNE VALADON

Vase of Flowers, Anemones in a White Vase,
date unknown

SUZANNE VALADON

Suzanne Valadon was born to an unmarried laundress on September 23, 1865. Her mother earned very little, and by the time Valadon was a teenager, she supported herself by doing a variety of jobs. She even performed as a circus acrobat until she was 16, when she got badly hurt falling from a trapeze. Looking for a safer occupation, she became an artists' model.

Valadon posed for some of the most important painters of the day. She can be seen dancing in two of Renoir's masterpieces and appears in several by Lautrec. She never had money for art lessons but learned to paint by observing the artists she modeled for.

At the time, there were very few professional women artists. In 1894, she was the first woman to be admitted in the Société Nationale des Beaux-Arts, which was a major accomplishment. Valadon showed her work in many exhibitions and became internationally known. Her son, Maurice Utrillo, became a well-known artist too.

art. She was glad he had found something that made him happy.

When it came time to choose an art school, Princeteau suggested he attend the classes of one of the most famous portrait painters in France—Léon Bonnat. Shortly after Henri started, however, Bonnat closed his studio, so the aspiring artist decided to study with Fernand Cormon.

Although Cormon's style of painting was more traditional than he liked, Lautrec enjoyed his classes. He liked the company of the other students, too. Lautrec's personality was larger than life; he was witty and gregarious and loved being the center of attention. The studio provided him the perfect stage. He was a good student and followed Cormon's instructions, but when Cormon wasn't within earshot Lautrec would entertain his classmates with outrageous songs and jokes.

Even though he came from an aristocratic family, Lautrec was very down to earth. His classmates appreciated his generous, affectionate nature. He made many friends, including Émile Bernard. Early in 1886, Vincent van Gogh joined the class. Although they were exact opposites, Henri and Vincent became good friends. At night, a gang including Lautrec, van Gogh, and Bernard often met at one of the neighborhood cabarets. Lautrec made a pastel portrait of van Gogh sitting at one of their hangouts.

For several months Lautrec shared an apartment with another student at Cormon's, Albert Grenier.

Much to his delight, the Impressionist artist Edgar Degas had a studio in the same building, across the courtyard. Lautrec was a huge fan of Degas. It must have thrilled him to know he was working under the same roof as the master.

A COLORFUL CHARACTER

After attending Cormon's class for five years, Lautrec decided to work on his own. He rented a huge studio and stuffed it with art supplies and oddities.

There wasn't an empty corner in the place. Visitors found a jumble of easels supporting unfinished paintings, stools, ladders, and piles of cardboard. Lautrec enjoyed this untidiness and wouldn't allow anyone to touch or move anything. There were two enormous tables on opposite sides of the room. One near the door was covered with liquor bottles and bartending equipment. Lautrec concocted exotic cocktails for all his guests whether they wanted them or not. The second table was heaped with all sorts of interesting objects. He'd pull items from the pile to show his guests: a Japanese wig, a ballet slipper, or a silly hat. There might be an interesting photograph or a prisoner's love letter. He'd proudly present these with an amusing remark.

Like his father, Lautrec loved to dress up in eccentric costumes. He used every excuse to have a party where he could entertain friends with his outlandish antics.

When not entertaining at his studio, Lautrec arranged elaborate luncheons at his favorite restaurants.

101

He knew the specialties of every restaurant in Paris and insisted that each course be eaten at a different one. A friend remembered that at the end of one feast, the guests wondered what the perfect dessert would be. Lautrec got up and marched the group down the street, up three flights of steps, and into an apartment. Scarcely taking time to greet the people who lived there, he led the group to a portrait of the owner by Degas. "There's my dessert!" he said with a flourish. He couldn't think of a better treat than a painting by Degas.

Like Degas, Lautrec wanted to portray scenes of Parisian life. Cabaret singers, circus performers, and people out having a good time were his favorite subjects. Landscapes and still lifes didn't interest him at all. Unlike most of his artist friends, Lautrec didn't have to earn an income by selling his art. This allowed him to paint as he pleased and experiment with new ideas.

Downstairs from his studio, one of his favorite models lived with her mother and son. Her name was Suzanne Valadon. Art lovers might recognize her face, if not her name. She appears in many Impressionist paintings, as she also modeled for Renoir and others.

At the time, most people didn't know that she was an artist, too. Valadon and Lautrec were good friends, and she would often pop upstairs to visit him. One day he unexpectedly dropped in on her and found her working on a drawing. When he saw how good the drawing was, he encouraged her to continue.

THE MOULIN ROUGE

Lautrec's studio was in the Montmartre section of Paris. Other artists, like van Gogh, lived there too. There was lots of nightlife, with cabarets, cafés, and dance halls. Lautrec visited them all. He could be seen chatting with friends and drinking while sketching the scenes around him. Back in his studio, he used the sketches to create a painting or a type of print called a lithograph.

His favorite place to draw was the Moulin Rouge. The little man with bowler hat and pince-nez glasses could be found there night after night at his reserved table. Everything he liked about Parisian night life was at the Moulin Rouge: bright lights and color, animated crowds, fantastic dancing, lively music, and the presence of friends. People who came early enjoyed a concert of funny or dramatic songs sung by Paris's top singers. Later the best dancers of Montmartre took the stage to perform the quadrille, a variation of the cancan.

The quadrille was a lively dance performed by four people: two men and two women. There was rivalry, especially between the women, over who could kick the highest (and display the most lacy underclothing). One famous dancer nicknamed La Goulue (French for "The Glutton"), was known for kicking off her partner's top hat, then landing in the splits. Her favorite partner was Valentin le Désossé ("Valentine the Boneless"). No-Bones Valentine was so flexible he seemed to be made of rubber. He was unbelievably tall and very thin.

MOULIN ROUGE, LA GOULUE

Lautrec was 26 when he designed this poster, and it made him famous overnight. He knew it would be pasted up outdoors and had to grab the attention of the person on the street. To be successful, it had to make an immediate and forceful impact.

To him, La Goulue was the most powerful symbol of the Moulin Rouge. In his design, viewers can't miss her red stockings and white petticoats. Her partner, Valentine the Boneless, draws our attention to her, along with the black silhouettes of the audience.

Other objects in the poster are important, too. Lautrec included the yellow balls on the left to represent the yellow globes of the modern electric chandeliers that hung over the dance floor. The yellow shape caused passersby to stop and take a second look, wondering, "What in the world is that?"

When Lautrec signed his piece in the lower left corner, he combined his initials, *HT*, with Lautrec. It's a bit confusing; one artist thought the name was Hautrec, an unknown artist. This wasn't an accident. Lautrec knew that when his father and family learned that their noble name appeared on a poster, they'd be outraged. To them, it was scandalous. Posters, after all, were not considered fine art. They were printed on cheap paper and pasted up by the thousands all over Paris, left to disintegrate in the rain. Some were even made into sandwich boards and paraded along Paris's most elegant avenue, the Champs-Élysées, on a donkey.

Lautrec signed his work several different ways during his career. Rearranging the letters in his name, he signed earlier paintings "Treclau." Eventually, he used "H T Lautrec," "Lautrec," or simply "HTL."

HENRI DE TOULOUSE-LAUTREC

Moulin Rouge, La Goulue, 1891

103

HENRI DE TOULOUSE-LAUTREC

Ambassadeurs: Aristide Bruant, 1892

Dressed in his black frock coat, with a silk top hat tipped over his eyes, he looked like an undertaker out for a night on the town. Their performances drew immense crowds and were greeted with wild applause.

THE POSTER WIZARD

The Moulin Rouge couldn't have had better advertising than posters designed by their best customer, Toulouse-Lautrec. No one in 1891 would have predicted that his first one would become an overnight sensation. Within days, it was a collector's item. Featured in the press, it became the international symbol of Paris within a year.

Posters, which were hung all around town, were a very popular way to advertise. They were usually filled with text and ornate images. Lautrec's poster was daringly original: an uncluttered, bold image told the story. Using very little text, he conveyed the excitement of the dance hall. His works were so popular that fans tore them off the walls before the glue could dry.

Entertainers commissioned Lautrec to design promotional posters, too. One of Lautrec's favorite singers was Aristide Bruant. He was known for his razor-sharp voice and his songs about life in the working-class suburbs. While performing he would leap up on customers' tables to belt out one of his hard-hitting songs. Lautrec was very familiar with Bruant's music. While at Cormon's studio he often entertained fellow students by singing Bruant songs during class.

The Art of the Poster

Toulouse-Lautrec knew that a successful poster had to make an immediate and forceful impact. Design a poster using his methods.

MATERIALS

Pencil

Eraser

9-by-12-inch piece of white construction paper

Markers

1. Lautrec's poster of Aristide Bruant contains very few elements: a simplified image of the singer, a headline, and a small amount of text. Keep this in mind when you design your own poster.

2. Decide what you'd like to advertise. It might be an announcement for an event, like a bake sale or concert.

3. Think of one bold graphic that best represents what you are advertising. For example, an ad for a winter concert could have an image of a cello wearing a scarf. A cherry-topped cupcake could advertise a bake sale.

4. Make a pencil sketch of your design on a piece of construction paper. Begin by drawing a line from the top of the paper to the bottom to divide the page into a left column with a width of two-thirds of the page and a right column one-third of the page wide. Lautrec used this layout to add interest to his design.

5. Place your graphic element a bit to the left of center on the page. Draw the image very large, so that it covers a big section of the paper. Allow space for text at the top and lower right of the page.

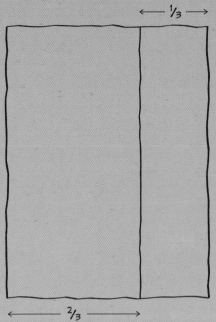

6. Think of one or two words that best announce your event, and write them in large outlined letters at the top of the page, filling the width of the paper.

7. Add the details about your event in the lower right corner. This text could include where the event will be held and when. Keep the message simple, and make the text large enough to be read from a distance.

8. Color the poster using bold, flat color. Leave areas that you'd like to be white uncolored. But be sure to color the background; this will make your graphic element stand out. Sign your poster in the lower left corner.

ART DETECTIVE

How to Spot a Toulouse-Lautrec

Here are some characteristics that help distinguish Toulouse-Lautrec's work:

❋ **Posters!** Of Parisian entertainment at the turn of the 20th century

❋ **Dancers!** White ruffled petticoats and high-kicking legs

❋ **Cabaret Crowds!** Enjoying a night out at the Moulin Rouge

When Bruant was hired to sing at Les Ambassadeurs, he chose Lautrec to design the promotional poster. The singer was known for his bold costumes and often appeared wearing a red scarf, black cape, and wide-brimmed hat. That is how Lautrec depicted him. The manager of the club had agreed to pay for the poster, but when he saw Lautrec's design, he rejected it. Les Ambassadeurs drew a sophisticated audience, and the manager thought Lautrec's poster was unappealing. Bruant disagreed. He refused to perform unless the poster was plastered all over Paris and displayed onstage.

Lautrec's commercial work wasn't limited to posters. He also designed theater programs, covers for sheet music, and book jackets.

THE FINAL YEARS

Lautrec led a full and busy life. His work appeared in many exhibitions, and he received numerous commissions. But after 17 years of making nightly rounds of the cabarets, dance halls, and bars of Montmartre, often drinking to excess, his health began to fail. In 1899, at the age of 34, he had a mental breakdown, and his mother committed him to a private asylum.

The clinic had once been a palace and included a wooded park with paths for patients to stroll. After a few days under the doctors' care, Lautrec began to feel better. He started drawing and socializing again, inviting his many friends to visit him.

Although he felt better, his doctors told him he wasn't well enough to leave the asylum. It wasn't long before he felt like a prisoner, and he devised a plan to get released. His plan consisted of two parts. He would stop complaining and act cheerful around the doctors and guards. Meanwhile, he would produce such great works of art that they would see he was sane.

Over the following weeks, Lautrec drew a series of circus scenes and portraits of other patients. Keeping in mind the audience he wanted to impress, he avoided his usual flamboyant style and lively scenes of merrymaking. The pictures he produced were calm, conservative, and colored with soft tones. After three months, the doctors

Paris Shadow Theater

Lautrec liked to visit a cabaret in Paris called Le Chat Noir to see shadow plays. Designed by artist Henri Rivière, the shadow theater there featured cut-out figures that were lit from behind. Their shapes drifted across a white silk screen as a story unfolded, accompanied by live music and narration. Sometimes as many as 20 people assisted Rivière during a performance. His stage was two stories high and took up an entire wall!

Make a minitheater and entertain your friends with your own shadow plays.

MATERIALS

Large square-shaped shoe box

Scissors

Construction paper, several colors plus black

Glue stick

Thin white paper

Masking tape

Flashlight or small reading lamp

Pencil

Bamboo skewers

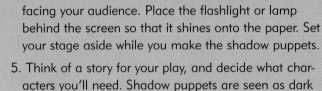

1. Cut a large square hole in the bottom of the shoe box.

2. Decorate the outside of the box with designs cut from construction paper and glued in place.

3. Cut a square of white paper that it is ½ inch larger on all sides than the hole in the shoe box, and tape it to the inside of the box, covering the hole. This is your screen.

4. Position the box on its side, with the paper screen facing your audience. Place the flashlight or lamp behind the screen so that it shines onto the paper. Set your stage aside while you make the shadow puppets.

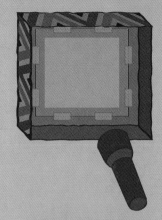

5. Think of a story for your play, and decide what characters you'll need. Shadow puppets are seen as dark shapes and do not have many details. Plan how you would draw them so that their outlines give enough detail. You may also need to make shadow props, like trees or houses.

6. Draw each puppet or prop on black paper. If you like, add simple details like eye holes or windows inside the shapes.

7. Cut the shapes out.

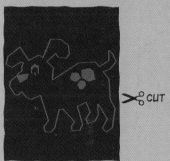

8. Form a 2-inch piece of masking tape into a sticky ball. Press the pointed end of a skewer into the ball, then stick it to the cutout. Repeat for each shape.

9. Perform the play in a dark room with your flashlight or lamp switched on. Hold the shape up to the screen from inside the box, and move it as needed for your story. Change or add puppets as you tell your story.

BALL OF MASKING TAPE

SKEWER

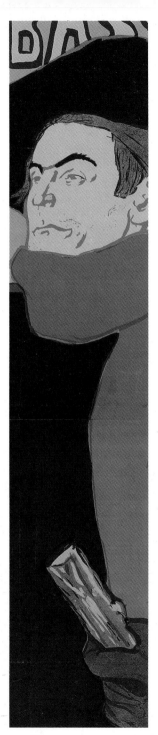

released him. "I bought my freedom with my drawings," he proudly announced.

Lautrec tried to live a healthier life after his release. His friends helped by discouraging his old habits, and for a while he seemed focused and productive. But he eventually began drinking again. He suffered a stroke in the spring of 1901. That September, Lautrec died at his mother's home at age 36.

WHAT LAUTREC LEFT BEHIND

Henri de Toulouse-Lautrec was one of the most innovative artists of the late 19th century. Despite his short life, he was enormously productive. He revolutionized the art of the poster, made more than 300 lithographs, and painted some 600 canvases that celebrate Paris nightlife at the turn of the 20th century.

After Lautrec's death, his art dealer, Maurice Joyant, and his mother promoted his work. The countess contributed funds for a museum to be built in Albi, the city in southern France where he was born. Today, the Musée Toulouse-Lautrec houses the paintings she inherited after Lautrec's death, as well as all 31 of his posters. Work by other artists of his time, including Suzanne Valadon and Edgar Degas, are also displayed.

PAUL SIGNAC

The Harbor of St. Tropez, 1893

8 Paul Signac

PAUL SIGNAC WAS A PAINTER, sailor, and promoter . . . of dots. Although Georges Seurat is the most famous Pointillist artist, Signac was the most vocal. Much of what we know about Pointillism and the artists who experimented with the colorful dabs and dots comes from Signac's writings.

SIGNAC'S CHILDHOOD

Paul Victor-Jules Signac was born in Paris on November 11, 1863. His father owned a prosperous harness and saddle business that supplied Emperor Napoléon III.

Shortly after Paul's birth, the Signacs moved to the artists' quarter, Montmartre, where they lived above their shop. It was an interesting place for a boy to grow up. When walking to school, he passed art studios and galleries whose windows were filled with paintings. His favorites were brightly colored and created by the young artists who called themselves Impressionists. Their art was very modern; Paul was only 10 when they held their first exhibition. At the time, they weren't really appreciated. Most people thought their canvases looked messy and unfinished. But young Paul liked them.

When he was 16, he went to see the Impressionists' fifth exhibition. The two most famous Impressionists, Claude Monet and Pierre-Auguste Renoir, didn't have work in the show. But many others, like Camille Pissarro, Gustave Caillebotte, and Paul Gauguin, had pieces on display. Admiring a painting by Edgar Degas, Paul pulled out a notebook and started to sketch it. Making sketches of masterpieces was a tradition in Paris. Art students flocked to the Louvre to copy the masters. But Gauguin spotted him, marched over, and chastised him. "One does not copy here, sir," he informed the boy and threw him out of the exhibit. Long after, Signac loved to

recount the story. Luckily it didn't dampen his enthusiasm for art.

That same year, tragedy struck when Paul's father died of tuberculosis. His mother decided to sell their business and move to the suburbs. The sale of the business provided Paul with a secure income for the rest of his life and freedom to do as he pleased. His mother would have liked him to be an architect, but she didn't insist. Although he was an excellent student and loved literature, he left school to take up painting.

Soon after, an exhibition of Monet's paintings made a huge impact on him. He was convinced he wanted to become an Impressionist.

AN ARTIST WITH MANY INTERESTS

Signac's new home was in Asnières, a suburb northwest of Paris. He lived near the banks of the Seine, near beautiful beaches where Parisians came to relax on Sunday afternoons and artists came to paint. Unlike most aspiring artists, Signac did not enroll in art school. To him, being an Impressionist meant painting outside, not in a stuffy studio. So he took his paints to the riverside to practice on his own. It was there that he met Gustave Caillebotte, an Impressionist whose hobby was sailing. They went sailing together, and it wasn't long before Signac bought his own boat.

The following summer, Signac visited the Normandy coast and painted his first seascapes. He later described his Impressionist technique of those early years. "I did

them by smearing on reds, greens, blues, and yellows without much care but with enthusiasm." Perhaps he realized art lessons weren't such a bad idea after all. When he returned from the coast, he enrolled in an art class run by Émile Bin. He only stayed a short time, and perhaps the best thing to come of it was meeting Père Tanguy, who came to sell paint to the students. Signac became a regular visitor to Tanguy's shop. He admired his collection of modern paintings and even persuaded his own mother to buy a landscape by Cézanne. Years later, he met his good friend Vincent van Gogh there.

Signac was very outgoing and made friends easily. He came in contact with several novelists, poets, and critics. A talented writer himself, he joined in their discussions about literature, politics, and art. One journalist in the group, Félix Fénéon, became a strong supporter of the painting technique that Signac was soon to adopt from a new friend, Georges Seurat.

MEETING SEURAT

Signac was 21 when he met Georges Seurat, the artist who would change his life. They both had paintings in an exhibition called the Salon des Artistes Indépendants. When Signac and Seurat happened to sit next to each other during a meeting to plan future exhibits, they struck up a friendship even though they had very different personalities.

While Signac was extroverted and talkative, Seurat was calm and reserved. Their artistic backgrounds were

GEORGES SEURAT

GEORGES SEURAT WAS BORN IN PARIS in 1859. He started taking drawing lessons when he was 16 years old. At 18 he was admitted to the École des Beaux-Arts, one of the world's most prestigious art schools specializing in traditional art.

But Seurat was not a traditional artist. After his lessons he would climb the great staircase of the École and enter the library. There he'd read all he could about art and science. One of his favorite authors was Charles Blanc, who believed art could be created using a scientific method. After 18 months of study, Seurat quit the École, rented an art studio, and started experimenting with a style of his own.

Continuing his scientific research, he learned of a physicist in Scotland named James Clerk Maxwell, who showed how colors could be blended. Maxwell painted two colors on a disk, one on each side. When he spun the disk rapidly, the colors appeared to blend, creating a new color. A blue and yellow disk would look green.

An American physicist, Ogden Rood, thought that you didn't have to spin a disk. From a distance, small dots of different colors, when painted close to each other, blended together. This effect is called "optical mixing." From these experiments and others, Seurat developed a new painting technique. It all came down to a simple dot.

Seurat decided to paint entire pictures using small dots. Instead of mixing colors on his palette like other artists, he let the viewer's eye mix his dabs. Painting with small dots, or points, is called Pointillism. Seurat's most famous painting, *A Sunday on La Grande Jatte*, takes up an entire wall. He worked on this huge canvas, dot by tiny dot, for two years until it was finished.

When it came to his private life, Seurat never confided in his friends and didn't have much to say unless it was about his art. Even his closest friends didn't know he had a girlfriend named Madeleine Knobloch and that they had a baby son. Seurat's friends only learned about his small family after his unexpected death. He was only 31 years old when he became ill with fever and suddenly died. His artist friends, especially Paul Signac, carried on by writing about Seurat's ideas and creating their own paintings filled with vibrant dots of color.

GEORGES SEURAT

A Sunday on La Grande Jatte,
1884, 1884–86

also quite different. Seurat, who was four years older, had been trained at the famous École des Beaux-Arts. Signac, on the other hand, was mostly self-taught. The gregarious young artist was fascinated by his quiet new friend, who had some very interesting ideas.

It was a perfect match. Seurat's ideas about painting and formal training gave Signac the grounding he was searching for. In return, Signac introduced Seurat to his circle of literary and artistic friends. Two years later,

when Seurat exhibited his revolutionary style of painting, they were some of his biggest fans. While Seurat quietly sat on the sidelines, Signac enthusiastically explained his ideas and lobbied critics and journalists to write about them.

The painting that turned the art world upside down was Seurat's huge 7-feet-tall by 10-feet-wide painting, *A Sunday on La Grande Jatte.* Seurat started working on it soon after he met Signac. He began by making dozens

114

of studies at La Grande Jatte, a waterside park where Sunday boaters and courting couples spent lazy afternoons. Back at his studio, he prepared a canvas that was so large he had to use a ladder to reach its top. He patiently applied dot by tiny dot over the canvas until it was covered in shimmering color. A completely new method of painting was born.

Signac visited Seurat's studio often and began using his technique. Others tried it too, and when the Impressionists organized their last exhibition, Signac and Seurat were invited to participate.

DOTS UNVEILED

Even before the exhibition opened, the dots caused an uproar. Some Impressionists approved of the new additions. Camille Pissarro was so interested he created several dotted paintings of his own. He planned to exhibit his work in the show and insisted that Seurat and Signac be included. But others, like Monet, thought Seurat's approach undermined the effect Impressionists were trying to create. It was a very deliberate method, with each dab carefully placed. Monet preferred portraying a quick impression using spontaneous brush strokes. He was appalled that Seurat made more than 50 studies for *La Grande Jatte* before the final painting.

After many heated arguments, threats, and compromises, the Eighth (and last) Impressionist Exhibition opened its doors on May 15, 1886. Although the organizers set the "offending" art apart in its own room, Monet and Renoir boycotted the show. They refused to be associated with Seurat's new technique, which to them was more about science than art. Dotted paintings irritated some art lovers but drew a great deal of attention from younger critics. One, Félix Fénéon, admiringly dubbed the new style of painting Neo-Impressionism. Later it was called Pointillism.

MEETING VAN GOGH

Van Gogh had been living in Paris for three months by the time the Eighth Impressionist Exhibition opened. He was already dazzled by the brightly colored canvases of the Impressionists. The Neo-Impressionists' art opened even more possibilities. When he ran into Signac at Tanguy's shop and heard his theories about color, van Gogh was ready to try them out. But van Gogh wasn't patient enough to fill a canvas with carefully considered dots. Instead, he used large dabs and dashes of paint, which made his paintings have an energy all their own.

Signac enjoyed van Gogh's company, and they often painted together outdoors. They both were talkers and sometimes got so involved in their conversation they forgot what they were doing. Signac liked to tell the story of walking home from one outing with van Gogh. The Dutchman waved his arms around so much during one of their discussions that he covered himself and passersby with paint from the wet canvas he was carrying. Occasionally, another artist, Émile Bernard, would join

them. Signac and Bernard could be hot-headed about their artistic beliefs. Sometimes they'd start quarreling, and van Gogh, who wasn't so calm himself, would have to mediate.

When van Gogh moved to Arles, he and Signac kept in touch through letters. They discussed their ideas about color and included sketches of what they were working on. One year later, Signac was able to see van Gogh's work in person while traveling to the Mediterranean. At this time van Gogh was hospitalized in Arles, being treated for his breakdown. Signac persuaded the doctors to release him for the day so they could visit van Gogh's house and see his paintings. Signac wanted to help his tormented friend and suggested they paint together at the coast. Realizing he was too sick, van Gogh declined.

Signac's visit meant a great deal to van Gogh. When he left, van Gogh gave him a painting of two herrings. Soon after, he sent a letter thanking Signac for the visit that "helped lift my spirits."

Nine months later, Signac was able to see six of van Gogh's canvasses, including two luminous paintings of sunflowers, when they were both invited to show their work at an exhibit in Brussels. By then van Gogh was in an asylum and could not leave. He missed an exciting night that was ignited by his paintings.

Signac, Toulouse-Lautrec, and other participants traveled to Brussels to attend a banquet before opening night. During the evening, Lautrec overheard a Belgian painter, Henry de Groux, insulting van Gogh's work.

De Groux was angry because his work would be shown next to the "abominable Pot of Sunflowers by Monsieur Vincent." When de Groux called van Gogh an ignoramus and a show-off, Lautrec had heard enough! Though ready to clobber de Groux with his cane, Lautrec instead challenged him to a duel. Signac, who could turn on his fiery temper when needed, came to Lautrec's side. He threatened to kill de Groux if he hurt Lautrec. De Groux took back his criticism of van Gogh, and the duel was called off.

THE AVID SAILOR

Less than a year after van Gogh's death, Signac lost another friend. He was crushed when Seurat suddenly became ill with fever and died. He had lost not only his friend but the leader of their small group of artists. Now the job of keeping Neo-Impressionism alive was his. With the help of a few like-minded artists, he planned Neo-Impressionist exhibitions and continued to write articles. And he kept on painting.

Signac concluded that Pointillism was best used to depict sunshine and water—scenes that sparkled. He began to specialize in shimmering seascapes. It was the perfect subject for a sailor!

Signac loved the sea and was an avid sailor. Over his lifetime he owned 32 boats, and he spent much of his free time on the water. The summer of Seurat's death, he set sail in his 36-foot yacht, named in honor of *Olympia*, Édouard Manet's 1863 painting. He was a big

PAUL SIGNAC

Entrance to the Port of
Honfleur, 1899

fan of Manet. He pointed his *Olympia* toward St. Tropez, a beautiful town on France's Mediterranean coast.

For Signac, painting and sailing was a perfect combination. His sailor's eye saw details in the water, such as wavelets stirred by the breeze, that most people would miss. He included these little details in his paintings with colors that created shimmering water and dazzling skies. In St. Tropez he found the tranquility he needed to develop his art. "Happiness—that is what I have just discovered," he wrote in a letter to his mother. His brushwork became looser, more like mosaic squares than little dots.

For many years, Signac divided his time between St. Tropez and Paris. Several artists came to visit Signac during his stays in St. Tropez, including Henri Matisse. Just before his 30th birthday, Signac married his longtime friend Berthe Robles. They bought a home in St. Tropez and named it after a sailing term: La Hune. When he had met Robles 10 years earlier, she was a hatmaker.

Make a Pointillist Sailboat

Make a boat that looks like it sailed out of one of Signac's paintings. Sail your Pointillist creation in your bathtub, or challenge friends to race their boats against yours in a pool.

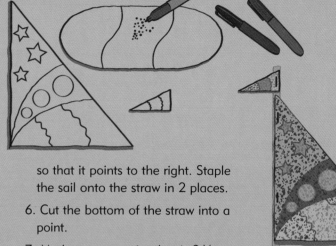

MATERIALS

9-by-12-inch sheet of white craft foam ⅛ inch thick

Pencil

Ruler

Scissors

Permanent markers

10-inch plastic straw

Stapler

Ballpoint pen

Tub of water

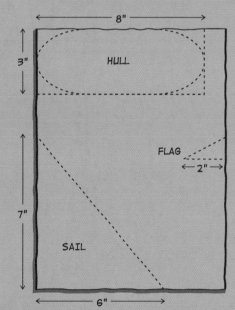

1. On a sheet of foam, draw a right-angle triangle that measures 6 inches along its base and 7 inches along its height. Cut the shape out. This is the sail of your sailboat.

2. Draw an 8-by-3-inch rectangle on the sheet of foam. Cut the shape out, and trim its ends into rounded points. This is the hull of your sailboat.

3. Cut a 2-inch-long pennant-shaped triangle from the foam. This is the flag.

4. Draw designs on the foam pieces in pencil. Color them in the Pointillist technique by pressing the point of the markers into the foam to make small dots. Color one side of the hull and both sides of the sail and flag.

5. Place the flag at the top of the straw so that it points left, and staple it onto the straw. Place the 7-inch length of the sail on top of the straw, below the flag,

so that it points to the right. Staple the sail onto the straw in 2 places.

6. Cut the bottom of the straw into a point.

7. Mark a center point that is 2½ inches from one end of the hull. Press the point of a pen into the mark to make hole.

8. Press the pointed end of the straw through the hole, inserting it 1 inch.

9. Float your sailboat in a tub of water.

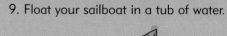

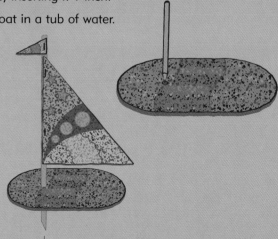

Over the years she modeled for many of his paintings. They later separated, and Signac started a family with Jeanne Selmersheim-Desgrange. They had a daughter named Ginette.

When he wasn't painting or writing, Signac sailed the *Olympia*. In 1929, he accepted a commission to sail into 100 French ports and paint watercolors of them. Signac thought it would take six months, but the project lasted two years.

WHAT SIGNAC LEFT BEHIND

Signac lived a long, productive, and happy life. His work was valued by collectors, and he sold many pieces during his lifetime. Along with the numerous paintings he created over his 55-year career, Signac wrote several important essays about art theory. In 1908 he become the president of the Société des Artistes Indépendants, which held exhibitions open to any artist who paid a small membership fee. Unlike with other exhibitions, paintings did not have to pass a jury selection. As a result, new styles could be seen by the public and other artists.

As the Neo-Impressionists' spokesman, Signac tried to persuade others to adopt Pointillism. Most of the artists who tried it, like van Gogh, moved on to other methods. But by experimenting they began thinking about color in a new way.

Signac's influence on the younger generation of artists was important. After Matisse painted together with

ART DETECTIVE

How to Spot a Signac

Here are some characteristics that help distinguish Signac's work:

❋ **Dots!** Portraits, landscapes, and harbor scenes made up of thousands of colorful dots

❋ **Sailboats!** He painted boats and the views seen from an onboard perspective: beaches and rocky coasts

❋ **Water and Sky!** For Signac, a shimmering seascape was the best use of the Pointillist technique

Signac, dabbling with dots, he took the experiment a step further. The result was a new style of painting called Fauvism.

Signac helped support the younger generation of artists, too. He bought paintings from Matisse and several others. He also bought works by the Impressionists he admired: Monet, Degas, and others.

The robust artist, writer, and promoter painted and sailed up until the last months of his life. He died in Paris in 1935 at the age of 71.

ÉMILE BERNARD

Breton Women with Parasols, 1892

9 Émile Bernard

WHEN IT CAME TO ART, Émile Bernard could do just about anything. He painted murals, designed tapestries, carved furniture, and painted windows so they looked like stained glass. He had a way with words, too. Give him a pen, and he would write a play, novel, or poem.

He was curious about everything. In later life, he interviewed and wrote about famous artists like Cézanne. He even published a magazine. Bernard isn't as well known today as some other artists. But through his writing we know more about them, including his good friend Vincent van Gogh.

BERNARD'S CHILDHOOD

Émile Henri Bernard was born on April 28, 1868, in Lille, France. Located in the north near the Belgian border, Lille is famous for its textile industry. For hundreds of years its weavers made fine fabrics for the French royalty. When the Industrial Revolution arrived in the 1800s, weaving was mechanized in huge factories. Émile's father had a successful business in the industry and hoped his son would eventually join him.

When Émile was three years old, his sister, Madeleine, was born. She was almost always sick and required their parents' constant attention. It seemed like they no longer had time for him. Luckily, his grandmother Sophie was there to help out.

Sophie was a successful businesswoman. She ran a laundry in Lille with more than 20 employees and rented rooms in her home to lodgers. She adored her grandson, who went to live with her when he was nine years old.

Lille had many places for Émile to explore. One of his favorites was an art studio that made stained glass windows. When held up to the light, the colors glowed.

Stained Glass Alphabet

Make your name glow! In this project you'll create dazzling letters to hang in a sunny window. Spell out your name, initials, or a special word.

MATERIALS

Pencil

Paper, 1 sheet for each letter

Clear acetate, 1 sheet for each letter

Clear tape

Acrylic or poster paints, colors plus black

Paintbrush

Container of water

Squeezable bottle of white glue, ½ to ¾ full

Spoon

Mixing stick

1. Think of the word or name you'd like to create. You'll make one piece of artwork for each letter.

2. Draw an outline of a large letter on the drawing paper. Decorate the letter with designs. For example, you could make large polka dots within it. Or add a simple design, like a butterfly, outside of the letter. Draw your designs in outline, like pictures in a coloring book.

3. Tape a piece of clear acetate on top of your letter design, and use a paintbrush to fill the outlined shapes with color. Let dry.

4. Add about a spoonful of black paint to the bottle of glue, stir it in, and replace the cap.

5. Squeeze the colored glue onto the acetate, outlining each color in the design. Let dry.

6. Repeat for each letter.

7. Gently remove the tape and arrange the letters on the acetate to create your word. Secure the letters to

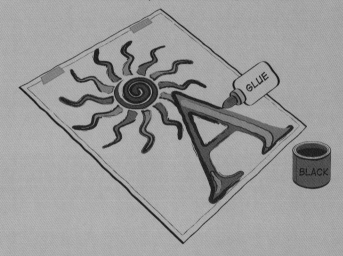

Later, Émile found his own way to make colors glow. When he was 15, he decorated the ceiling of his bedroom and painted designs on the windows. He filled the designs with color so his windows looked like they were made of stained glass.

THE DETERMINED ARTIST

When Émile was 10, his family moved to Paris. It was an exciting time to be in the city. The World's Fair was going on, and, among other delights, visitors could see the colossal head of the Statue of Liberty showcased in a garden. It was the work of sculptor Frédéric Auguste Bartholdi. When completed, it would be shipped to the United States as a gift from the people of France.

Each morning, Émile took lessons at the École des Arts Décoratifs before going to his regular school. The École specialized in the design of decorative pieces, like tapestries and embroidered pillows. Students were taught how to design pieces that could be produced by a machine. Along with being attractive, the designs had to adapt to the machines' limitations. His teachers stressed using geometric patterns. Émile, however, had his own ideas. When he refused to follow his teacher's instructions, he was expelled from the school. It wouldn't be the last time he caused trouble in class. Émile was very headstrong when it came to art.

He was determined to be an artist. Over the next few years, he copied well-known pictures by working from prints. Whenever he visited an art museum, he

Head of the Statue of Liberty on display in a park in Paris

brought along a sketchpad. To his father's horror, when Émile was 16 he announced that he wanted to be a painter. Mr. Bernard thought his son should be a businessman like him. They argued about it, but Émile won. In September, he began his training. The small, thin teenager with large dark eyes was accepted at the studio of Fernand Cormon.

Émile's classmates were a talented group. Some of them, like Toulouse-Lautrec, would become famous. One day, a new student joined the class—Vincent van Gogh.

123

For two years, Émile followed Cormon's instructions as best he could. But one day, when the class was painting a female model standing in front of a rust-colored curtain, he could no longer restrain himself. Instead of keeping the background plain, so the subject stood out, Émile decided to add bright red stripes. Cormon was a tolerant man, but this was too much. He insisted that Émile change it. When he refused, Cormon threw him out of class for "insubordinate behavior." When Émile's father found out that he had been expelled, he took his son's paintbrushes and threw them in the fire. If he thought that was going to stop him, he was mistaken. Émile's days as an artist had just begun.

A JOURNEY WEST

The spirited 18-year-old decided to study on his own by taking a six-month tour of the French countryside—on foot. Equipped with an array of art supplies that he had gotten on credit from Père Tanguy, he set off for western France. His plan was to explore the regions of Normandy and Brittany, sketching the landscape and painting canvases along the way. He was especially interested in visiting medieval cathedrals to see their stained glass windows.

He was enchanted by what he found. Brittany was a remote place where people spoke their own Celtic language and dressed in a way that hadn't changed since the Middle Ages. Émile Bernard was thrilled with their customs, dress, and way of living.

Along his journey, he ran into many other artists. They came from all over the world to paint the wild landscapes of Brittany. When Bernard reached the southern coast, he passed through the village of Pont-Aven. The charming river town by the sea, with its narrow cobbled lanes and stone houses, was a haven for artists.

A LASTING FRIENDSHIP

Bernard had completed many paintings by the time he returned to Paris that autumn. When he brought them to Tanguy's store, who should pop out of the back room but his old classmate, Vincent van Gogh!

Van Gogh had also left Cormon's class, rejecting the old-fashioned ideas. He had a studio in the apartment he shared with his brother Theo and was trying to learn on his own, like Bernard. Both artists were experimenting with bold brushstrokes, like the Impressionists, and little dots, like the Pointillists. Ultimately, they wanted to create a style of their own.

Over the next year and a half, they collaborated by painting together and visiting other artists' studios. Van Gogh shared his enthusiasm for Japanese prints with Bernard and took him to a gallery to see them.

Bernard's parents were not happy about his artistic endeavors. But he still had the loving support of his grandmother. When Sophie moved to Paris to live with the family, she had a studio built for him in their garden. His sister, Madeleine, was delighted to have an artist in the family. Later, she remembered how nice it was

Write an Acrostic Poem

Here's how to write a type of poem called an acrostic.

MATERIALS

Pencil

2 pieces of paper

An acrostic poem uses the first letter of each line to spell out a word. For example, if the word is "dots," the first line of the poem would begin with the letter *D*. The second line with the letter *O*, the third with *T*, and the fourth with *S*. Each line of the poem should relate to or describe the word.

For example, here's a poem about Signac's paintings, titled "Dots":

Dancing dabs

Of dazzling color

Together they shimmer and

Shine.

1. Think of a word that you'd like to use as the subject of your poem. The word might be your favorite color or something about your favorite artist. Write your subject word at the top of a piece of paper.

2. Under your subject word, list at least ten words or phrases that describe your subject. For example, with van Gogh in mind, words and phrases relating to "stars" could be: shimmer, shine, sailing in the sky, painted by van Gogh, light up the sky, in the night, glowing.

3. On a separate piece of paper, write your subject word down the left side of the page.

4. Use your list of words and phrases to help write a line for each letter in your word. Remember that each line should relate to your subject.

Here's an acrostic poem titled "Stars":

Sailing above

They shimmer and glow

Awaiting van Gogh.

Ready to be painted, they

Smile brightly.

ÉMILE BERNARD

Breton Women in a Green Pasture, 1888

to spend time with her brother in his studio when he asked her to pose. Sometimes van Gogh painted there too, as when they both painted portraits of Père Tanguy.

Because van Gogh was 15 years older than Bernard, he assumed the role of an older brother, giving him all sorts of advice. He defended him, too. When he met Bernard's father at the studio one day, they got into a terrible quarrel. Van Gogh told him Bernard had real talent and should be supported. Bernard's father disagreed, making van Gogh furious. He stormed out with Tanguy's wet portrait under his arm—and never came back.

When van Gogh organized an exhibition featuring several artists, he was thrilled that Bernard sold his first painting there. In February, van Gogh left for Arles. The day before, he and Bernard arranged his apartment just so, hoping Theo might somehow feel his brother still lived there.

Van Gogh hoped that someday Bernard would visit him in Arles. Until then, he promised to write. They exchanged many letters. Bernard also wrote poetry and often included his latest poems, which van Gogh took the liberty to critique. Along with giving advice about writing, he told Bernard what to eat and how to run his love life. Bernard must not have minded the unsolicited advice, because he always wrote back. And he saved all the letters.

PONT-AVEN

Van Gogh was determined to bring his artist friends together. He thought everyone would benefit if they painted side by side and shared ideas. He hoped to create a "Studio of the South" just for this purpose. Meanwhile, many of the artists he admired were already together in Pont-Aven. In his letters from Arles, he persistently nagged Bernard to join the artists there. Gauguin was there, having just returned from Martinique. He was sure something great would happen if Gauguin and Bernard painted together. When Bernard finally decided to go to Pont-Aven, van Gogh was thrilled.

Van Gogh was right; it turned out to be a very productive summer for both artists. In Paris, Bernard and another Cormon student, Louis Anquetin, had been experimenting with a new technique. The idea came from the stained glass windows Bernard loved. Instead of using loose, bold brushstrokes like the Impressionists or little dots of color like the Pointilists, Bernard used flat, colored shapes. These were darkly outlined, so his paintings looked a bit like a page from a coloring book. They also resembled a technique used in a type of jewelry called cloisonné. The style became known as Cloisonnism.

At Pont-Aven, Bernard shared his ideas with Gauguin. Twenty years older, Gauguin took on the role of master artist when he met "young Bernard." But Bernard had a lot of his own ideas. "Young Bernard is here and has brought some interesting things with him," Gauguin wrote in a letter to van Gogh. "He is one person who is not afraid to try anything."

Pont-Aven and its surrounding countryside provided all sorts of images to paint. The women, who still wore traditional costumes topped with big white bonnets called *coiffes*, were a favorite subject. But Bernard's portrayal was different from anything done before. In *Breton Women in a Green Pasture*, he set them in a solid lime-green field. He didn't include shadows in the picture, and the women's flat shapes seem to float, like a cutout. His painting resembled a cross between a stained glass window and a Japanese print. When Gauguin saw it, he was very impressed. Within a week or two, Gauguin painted a somewhat similar piece, *The Vision After the Sermon*. The colors in his painting were even brighter.

Instead of a green field, his grass was red. He added an angel wrestling with a man, too.

Both artists thought they should use their imaginations when painting a picture. If painting the grass red made it more dramatic, so be it. In Gauguin's painting, red symbolized the women's emotions as they witnessed the scene. Also, it wasn't important that objects were drawn to scale or in perspective. Lines, patterns, and

My dear Bernard,

I am very pleased you have joined Gauguin. . . . . How much I would like to spend these days in Pont-Aven; however, I find comfort in contemplating the sunflowers.

Sincerely yours,
Vincent

— Letter from Vincent van Gogh to Émile Bernard (excerpt), Arles, on or about August 21, 1888

brilliant color—that's what mattered. By sharing ideas, Bernard and Gauguin created a new way of painting. Later, Gauguin took all the credit, which made Bernard very angry.

That summer, Bernard's mother and sister joined the group in Pont-Aven. Madeleine loved Brittany and its customs. Like her brother, she was fascinated by the medieval art and architecture. There were many

MADELEINE IN THE BOIS D'AMOUR

IN *MADELEINE IN THE BOIS D'AMOUR*, Bernard painted his sister reclining in the woods. Madeleine's pose may seem odd, but Bernard positioned her that way to symbolize her enthusiasm for Brittany and the Middle Ages.

Her pose resembles a medieval effigy tomb, or *gisant*. During the Middle Ages, when someone of importance died, like a queen, they were buried inside a cathedral. Their image was carved in stone and set on top of their tomb. Bernard and Madeleine would have seen many *gisants* in the cathedrals they visited in Brittany.

ÉMILE BERNARD

Madeleine in the Bois d'Amour, 1888

beautiful sites to explore. On the edge of town, a forest with a lovely name, Bois d'Amour, was nestled along the banks of the River Aven. In a life-sized portrait, Bernard posed Madeleine as if resting in the woods and called it *Madeleine in the Bois d'Amour.*

GREETINGS FROM ARLES

Van Gogh kept in touch with the artists in Pont-Aven with long, detailed letters. He wished he could join them but was busily painting in Arles. In addition, he was getting his house ready to welcome his first guest, Gauguin.

In October, Bernard and Gauguin packed up their finished paintings and went their separate ways. Bernard went back to Paris. Gauguin was headed to the Yellow House in Arles. With his permission, Gauguin took along Bernard's *Breton Women in a Green Pasture* to show their friend. Van Gogh was so impressed when he saw the painting, he made a copy of it in watercolor to send to Theo. "It was so original I absolutely wanted to have a copy," he wrote to his sister Wil.

When Bernard heard that van Gogh was in an asylum, he sent a letter to art critic Albert Aurier. *"My dear friend Vincent is mad,"* he wrote. *"Since I heard that, I'm almost mad myself. . . . I have lost my best friend and one of the most wonderful and powerful minds I have known."*

Eight weeks later, van Gogh was in the hospital after cutting off part of his ear.

UNLUCKY IN LOVE

The following summer, Émile fell in love with a young girl named Charlotte Buisse. He wanted to marry her, but when Charlotte's father found out, he was not pleased. He demanded Émile prove he could earn enough on an artist's salary to support a family. Émile was living on a small allowance his father gave him. His paintings were starting to be displayed in exhibitions, but he wasn't earning a living from sales. He'd have to find a full-time job, and he knew just where to look.

The textile industry needed artists, so Émile moved back to Lille. He lived with his grandmother while working as a designer, making patterns called cartoons. Émile found the work incredibly boring. After six months, he quit and returned to Paris only to find Charlotte engaged to someone else.

Just when it seemed things couldn't get worse, Émile learned that van Gogh had killed himself. He arrived in Auvers in time to attend the funeral and help Theo arrange a memorial exhibition of his work.

EXPLORING THE PAST

Émile Bernard's next journey took him through Greece, Turkey, and the Holy Land. He began in Italy, where he was fascinated by Renaissance paintings. The paintings were realistic looking, with accurate colors and subjects that looked three dimensional.

How to Spot a Bernard

Here are some characteristics that help distinguish Bernard's work:

❋ **Coloring Book–Style!** Bright, flat colors outlined in black

❋ **Brittany Scenes!** Women in puffy white bonnets and large white collars

❋ **Tapestries, Stained Glass, Murals, Furniture!** Bernard used his coloring book–style and Brittany scenes in decorative pieces, too

Along his journey, he stopped long enough to make murals and decorative pieces for several churches. Finally, in Egypt, he settled in Cairo for 10 years. He married a Lebanese girl named Hanenah Saati and had five children. Sadly, three of them died from tuberculosis at a very young age.

When he was 36, Bernard's marriage ended. He returned to France with his two young children and a woman named Andrée Fort, whom he later married. He continued painting but was no longer an avant-garde artist. Seeing paintings centuries old had made a tremendous impact on Bernard. He changed his approach, trying to imitate the realistic styles of the 1500s. It was very different from what he had done before. Although he lived many more years, his days as a Post-Impressionist had ended.

A CREATIVE SPIRIT

Many people who knew "Bernard the artist" were not aware that the poems and stories they were reading were by "Bernard the writer." That's because he often used a false name ("nom de plume," or pen name) when he published them. But perhaps his most important stories were written using his real name and were about the artists he knew personally. He wrote about Gauguin, Cézanne, and others who are well known today. He even wrote a story about the art supply merchant who helped support them all, Père Tanguy. His articles appeared in several French magazines, including a journal he published himself.

He publicized his experience with van Gogh, too. After his friend's death, Bernard published the numerous letters Vincent had written to him. In them, van Gogh explains many of his concepts about painting.

WHAT BERNARD LEFT BEHIND

Émile Bernard died in Paris in 1941, a week before his 73rd birthday. When he was only 20 years old, he helped develop a style that other artists followed or modified for themselves. He was full of ideas and skilled at putting them into words. And he publicized other artists by writing about their lives and ideas.

Woven Styles

Bernard and Gauguin did not get along with Seurat and Signac. Members of each group believed so strongly in their own style of painting that the other's method annoyed them. In this project, you'll compare both styles, then weave them together for a dazzling piece that is uniquely your own.

MATERIALS

1 sheet of 9-by-12-inch white construction paper
Pencil
Acrylic or poster paints, several colors and black
Paintbrushes
Container of water
Cotton swabs
Scissors
Glue stick
1 sheet of 9-by-12-inch black construction paper

1. Fold the sheet of white construction paper in half so that it measures 9 by 6 inches.

2. Unfold the sheet of paper and place it horizontally. Using a pencil, draw a design made of large, simple shapes on the left half of the paper.

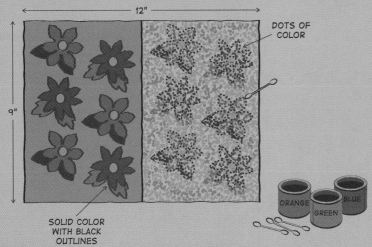

SOLID COLOR WITH BLACK OUTLINES

DOTS OF COLOR

ORANGE GREEN BLUE

3. Repeat the design on the right side of the paper, making it as similar as possible.

4. Paint one half of the paper using Bernard's technique: bright, flat colors outlined in black.

5. Paint the remaining half of the paper using Signac's technique: individual dots of color. Use cotton swabs dipped in paint to make the dots, one swab for each color. Let dry.

6. Study the two styles of painting you created, viewing them up close and from a distance. Which style do you prefer? Cut your artwork in half along the fold, separating the pieces.

7. Fold the picture painted with solid color in half, so that it measures 6 by 4 ½ inches. Starting at the folded edge, cut 3 or 4 slits into the sheet. Do not cut all the way through; stop about 1 inch from the end. Unfold and set aside.

8. Cut the picture made with dots into strips, cutting along its 9-inch length so that each strip is 6 inches long and about 1 inch wide. When finished, you'll have about 9 strips. Put aside the first and last strip that you cut—you will not use them.

9. Weave the strips through the slits of the solid-colored piece. The designs may or may not match up. The result will be a style uniquely your own.

10. Apply the glue stick to the back of your woven piece, and center it on a piece of black paper.

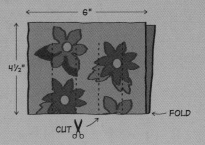

6"

4½"

FOLD

CUT

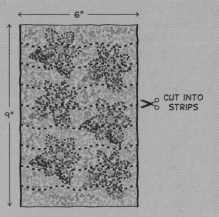

6"

9"

CUT INTO STRIPS

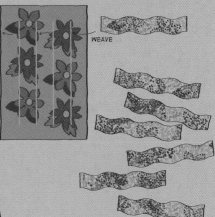

WEAVE

VINCENT VAN GOGH

Branch of an Almond Tree in
Blossom (detail), 1890

More Dazzling Than Ever

VINCENT VAN GOGH has been gone for more than 100 years, but his art lives on. Exhibitions of his work draw millions of visitors from around the world. It's hard to believe that his brilliant canvases filled with flowers, wheat fields, and starry nights were once ignored. His life has been portrayed in movies and songs. Just about everyone knows the name of the red-bearded artist who painted sunflowers.

His artist friends are more popular than ever too. Toulouse-Lautrec's posters and paintings of Parisian nightlife are widely recognized, as are Gauguin's brightly colored tropical scenes. Signac kept Pointillism alive long after its creator, Seurat, died. His luminous dot-filled paintings influenced the next generation of artists. Bernard's images of Brittany, done in bright colors outlined in black, inspired others as well. All the Post-Impressionists took what they learned from the Impressionists and went a step further. Bernard's extensive writing tells the story of how many of them did it.

Today, many Post-Impressionist paintings are considered masterpieces. They are shown in museums all over the world, waiting for you to visit them. Until then—visit them online! The Internet is full of interesting sites about the artists. Search their names, or go to www.carolbooks.net for links to wonderful sites and additional activities by this author.

POST-IMPRESSIONIST PATHS

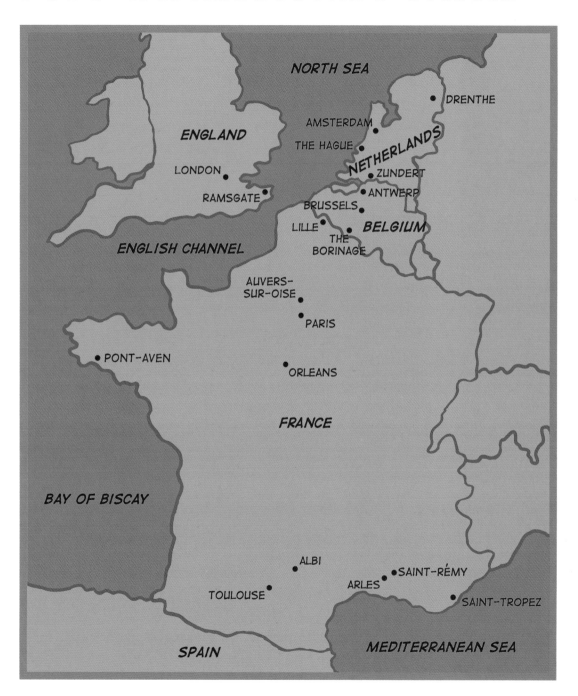

Glossary

absinthe: a green liqueur having a bitter anise or licorice flavor and a high alcohol content. Popular in van Gogh's time, absinthe is now prohibited in many countries because of its toxicity.

asylum: an institution for the care of people, especially those with physical or mental impairments.

cabaret: a restaurant or nightclub that provides programs of live entertainment.

Cloisonnism: a style of painting, created by Émile Bernard and others, where shapes are outlined in dark colors to create a two-dimensional, flat pattern.

color wheel: a circular arrangement of the primary colors (red, yellow, and blue) and their mixtures.

complementary colors: a pair of colors that sit opposite each other on the color wheel. When next to each other, each color makes the other seem more intense. Red and green, yellow and purple, and blue and orange are pairs of complementary colors.

connoisseur: a person with expert knowledge or training, especially in the fine arts.

cropping: cutting off the edge of a picture. Toulouse-Lautrec liked to use this technique.

Cubism: an art movement started around 1907 by Pablo Picasso and Georges Braque that breaks a picture down into geometric shapes. Images are depicted at many different angles at once.

digitalis: a plant of the genus *digitalis*, which includes the foxglove. The plant's seeds and dried leaves are used to make a drug that is used to prevent heart disease.

dike: a raised bed constructed to prevent flooding.

École des Beaux-Arts: French for "School of Fine Arts."

engraving: a printing technique. Vincent van Gogh sold the high-quality prints when he was an art dealer.

epilepsy: any of various neurological disorders characterized by sudden recurring attacks of motor, sensory, or psychic malfunction with or without loss of consciousness or convulsive seizures.

Expressionism: an artistic style in which the artist depicts not how a scene really looks but how he or she feels about the scene. This is accomplished through the distortion and exaggeration of shape and the vivid or violent application of color. Its roots are found in the works of Vincent van Gogh.

Fauvism: a style of art that began around 1905 and used brilliant colors to express emotion. Portraits, landscapes, and other motifs were painted in bright, unnatural colors. Henri Matisse was the leader of this movement, which lasted only a few years. The word *fauve* means "wild beast" in French.

fanatic: a person who has an extreme, unreasoning enthusiasm.

Flemish: of or relating to Flanders, a region that once included parts of northern France, western Belgium, and southwestern Netherlands.

Industrial Revolution: changes that were brought about when extensive mechanization of production systems resulted in a shift from home-based hand manufacturing to large-scale factory production.

Impressionism: a style of painting that was developed in France during the 1870s by Claude Monet and others. The painters concentrated on their immediate visual impression of a scene, using bright colors and unblended brushstrokes.

landscape: a picture of natural scenery.

lithography: a printing process in which the image to be printed is rendered on a flat surface, as on a large smooth stone or sheet of zinc, and treated to retain ink while the non-image areas are treated to repel ink. Toulouse-Lautrec used this technique.

Louvre (LOO-vruh): located in Paris, the Louvre is one of the largest and most famous art museums in the world. It was originally built as a residence for the king of France. Today it exhibits some of the world's greatest art treasures.

merchant marines: a nation's commercial ships.

Middle Ages: the period in European history between antiquity and the Renaissance, often dated from A.D. 476 to 1453. The art and architecture produced during this time is described as being Medieval.

mirror image: an image that has its parts arranged with a reversal of right and left, as it would appear if seen in a mirror. Many self-portraits are mirror images because the artist looked at him- or herself in a mirror when painting his or her own image.

mistral: a brief, violent windstorm that blows in southern France.

Neo-Impressionists: the name first given to the artists who painted using dots of color. These artists, such as Paul Signac and Georges Seurat, were later called Pointillists.

nobility: a class of persons distinguished by high birth or rank including dukes and duchesses and earls and countesses. Toulouse-Lautrec came from a long line of nobility.

nom de plume: French for "pen name," it is a fictitious name used by a writer.

perspective: the method used by artists to make a flat surface look as if it has depth.

Pointillism: the technique of placing tiny dots of pure color next to one another so that, from a distance, the viewer's eye mixes them together.

portrait: a picture or sculpture of a particular person.

Post-Impressionism: a school of painting in France in the late 19th century that went beyond Impressionism to use form and color in a more personally expressive way.

Renaissance: the period of European history at the close of the Middle Ages (often dated 1453) through the middle of the 17th century.

the Salon: a yearly or biyearly exhibition in Paris that featured artwork done in a traditional style. Because a jury selected the pieces to be shown, many of the modern painters, like the Impressionists, were excluded from the exhibition.

seascape: a picture featuring the sea.

self-portrait: a picture or sculpture that an artist makes of him- or herself.

still life: a picture of a group of inanimate objects arranged by the artist. It's usually set indoors and contains a manmade object, such as a tabletop or vase.

ukiyo-e: a Japanese term that means "pictures of the floating world," it is the name for Japanese woodblock prints, which were produced between the 17th and 20th centuries. The prints depict scenes of everyday interests such as kabuki actors, women in kimonos, and Japanese landscapes. They were greatly admired by van Gogh and other artists during his time.

Victorian: relating to the time when Victoria was queen of the United Kingdom (1837–1901). During this time, furnishings were very ornamental and featured heavy, lavish fabrics and ornately carved wood.

Bibliography

Bernard, Bruce. *Van Gogh: Explore Vincent van Gogh's Life and Art, and the Influences That Shaped His Work.* New York: Dorling Kindersley, 1992.

Cachin, Françoise. *Paul Signac.* Greenwich, CT: New York Graphic Society, 1971.

Ferretti-Bocquillon, Marina, Anne Distel, John Leighton, and Susan Alyson Stein. *Signac 1863–1935.* New York: Metropolitan Museum of Art/Yale University Press, 2001.

Frey, Julia Bloch. *Toulouse-Lautrec: A Life.* New York: Viking, 1994.

Gayford, Martin. *The Yellow House: Van Gogh, Gauguin, and Nine Turbulent Weeks in Arles.* New York: Little, Brown, 2006.

Greenberg, Jan, and Sandra Jordan. *Vincent van Gogh: Portrait of an Artist.* New York: Dell Yearling, 2001.

Greenfield, Howard. *First Impressions: Paul Gauguin.* New York: Harry N. Abrams, 1993.

Hintz, Martin. *The Netherlands* (Enchantment of the World series). Danbury, CT: Children's Press, 1999.

Jansen, Leo. *Vincent van Gogh, Painted with Words: The Letters to Émile Bernard.* New York: Rizzoli, 2007.

Mühlberger, Richard. *What Makes a van Gogh a van Gogh?* New York: Metropolitan Museum of Art/Viking, 1993.

Ozanne, Marie-Angélique, and Frédérique de Jode. *Theo: The Other Van Gogh.* New York: Vendome Press, 1999.

Pickvance, Ronald. *Van Gogh in Saint-Rémy and Auvers.* New York: Metropolitan Museum of Art/Harry N. Abrams, 1986.

Rewald, John. *The History of Impressionism.* New York: Museum of Modern Art, 1973.

——. *Post-Impressionism: From van Gogh to Gauguin.* New York: Museum of Modern Art, 1962.

——. *Studies in Post-Impressionism.* New York: Harry N. Abrams, 1986.

Sabbeth, Carol. *Monet and the Impressionists for Kids: Their Lives and Ideas.* Chicago: Chicago Review Press, 2002.

Saltzman, Cynthia. *Portrait of Dr. Gachet: The Story of a van Gogh Masterpiece.* New York: Penguin Books, 1998.

Stevens, Mary Anne. *Émile Bernard 1868–1941: A Pioneer of Modern Art.* Amsterdam: Van Gogh Museum/Waanders Publishers, 1990.

Wright, Lyndie. *Toy Theaters.* New York: Franklin Watts, 1991.

WORLD WIDE WEB:
"Van Gogh's Letters—Unabridged." WebExhibits. January 2010. www.webexhibits.org/vangogh/.

Image Credits

Page x
Vincent van Gogh
Sunflowers, 1888
oil on canvas
National Gallery, London,
    Great Britain
Photo Credit: © National Gallery,
    London / Art Resource, NY

Pages xiv and 72
Vincent van Gogh
Self-Portrait, 1889
oil on canvas
Photo: Gérard Blot
Musée d'Orsay, Paris, France
Photo Credit: Réunion des Musées
    Nationaux / Art Resource, NY

Page 3
Vincent van Gogh
The Siesta (after Millet), 1889–1890
oil on canvas
Photo: Hervé Lewandowski
Musée d'Orsay, Paris, France
Photo Credit: Réunion des Musées
    Nationaux / Art Resource, NY

Page 6
Vincent van Gogh
Letter to Paul Gauguin. Appendix 1,
    [ev:2] (711) Arles, Wednesday, 17
    October, 1888
Photo: Joseph Zehavi, 2007
Gift of Eugene V. Thaw in honor
    of Charles E. Pierce, Jr., 2007 Art
    Resource, NY
The Pierpont Morgan Library, New
    York, NY, U.S.A.
Photo Credit : The Pierpont Morgan
    Library / Art Resource, NY

Page 9
Vincent van Gogh
The Red Vineyard at Arles, 1888
oil on canvas
Pushkin Museum of Fine Arts,
    Moscow, Russia
Photo Credit: Erich Lessing /
    Art Resource, NY

Page 12
Vincent van Gogh
Head of a Peasant Woman, 1884
oil on canvas
Gift of Charles H. Yalem by exchange,
    and funds given by Bruce and
    Kimberly Olson, Mrs. Alvin R.
    Frank, Sam and Marilyn Fox and
    the Fox Family Foundation, Mr.
    and Mrs. Jack C. Taylor, Mr. and
    Mrs. Andrew C. Taylor, the Ruth
    Peters MacCarthy Charitable
    Trust, the Arthur and Helen Baer
    Charitable Foundation, Mr. and
    Mrs. David C. Farrell, the Jordan
    Charitable Foundation, Mr. and
    Mrs. Kenneth S. Kranzberg, Mr. and
    Mrs. Thomas K. Langsdorf, Mr. and
    Mrs. William C. Rusnack, and the
    Gary Wolff Family
Saint Louis Art Museum

Page 16
Vincent van Gogh
The Carrot Puller, 1885
black chalk (Bergkreide), with stumping
    and erasing on cream wove paper
Gift of Dorothy Braude Edinburg
    to the Harry B. and Bessie K. Braude
    Collection
Art Institute of Chicago

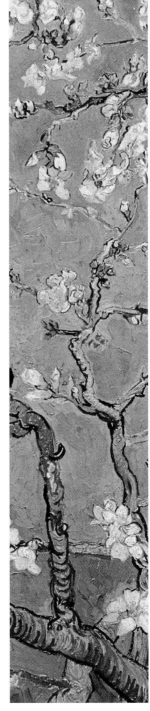

Page 55
Vincent van Gogh
The Bedroom, 1889
oil on canvas
Helen Birch Bartlett Memorial
    Collection
Photograph by Greg Williams
Art Institute of Chicago

Page 56
Paul Gauguin
Madame Roulin, 1888
oil on canvas
Funds given by Mrs. Mark C. Steinberg
Saint Louis Art Museum

Page 60
Vincent van Gogh
*Madame Roulin Rocking the Cradle
    (La Berceuse)*, 1889
oil on canvas
Helen Birch Bartlett Memorial
    Collection
Art Institute of Chicago

Page 63
Vincent van Gogh
Self-Portrait with Cut-off Ear and Bandage,
    1889
oil on canvas
Courtauld Institute Galleries, London,
    Great Britain
Photo Credit: Erich Lessing /
    Art Resource, NY

Pages 64 and 77 (detail)
Vincent van Gogh
Stairway at Auvers, 1890
oil on canvas
Saint Louis Art Museum

Page 67
Vincent van Gogh
The Starry Night, 1889
oil on canvas
29 x 36 ¼ in.
Acquired through the Lillie P. Bliss
    Bequest
Museum of Modern Art, New York,
    NY, U.S.A.
Photo Credit: Digital Image © The
    Museum of Modern Art/Licensed by
    SCALA / Art Resource, NY

Pages 74 and 132 (detail)
Vincent van Gogh
Branch of an Almond Tree in Blossom,
    1890
Van Gogh Museum, Amsterdam,
    The Netherlands
Photo Credit: Art Resource, NY

Page 76
Vincent van Gogh
Portrait of Dr. Gachet, 1890
Musée d'Orsay, Paris, France
Photo Credit: Scala / Art Resource,
    NY

Page 79
Vincent van Gogh
Wheatfield with Crows, 1890
Van Gogh Museum, Amsterdam,
    The Netherlands
Photo Credit: Art Resource, NY

Page 84
Paul Gauguin
Portrait of the Artist with the Idol,
    ca. 1893
oil on canvas
17 ¼ x 12 ⅞ in. (43.8 x 32.7cm)
Bequest of Marion Koogler McNay
McNay Art Museum, San Antonio,
    Texas, U.S.A.
Photo Credit: © McNay Art Museum /
    Art Resource, NY

Page 87
Paul Gauguin
Women Bathing, 1885
oil on canvas
National Museum of Western Art,
    Tokyo

Page 90
Paul Gauguin
The Vision After the Sermon, 1888
National Gallery of Scotland,
    Edinburgh, Scotland, Great Britain
Photo Credit: Art Resource, NY

Page 93
Paul Gauguin
Piti Teina (Two Sisters), 1892
oil on canvas
Hermitage Museum, St. Petersburg

Index

Page numbers in *italics* refer to pages with images.

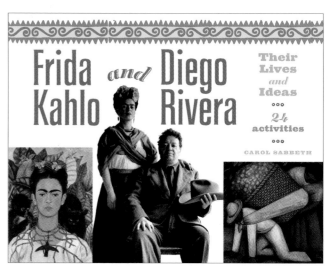